RICHARD MAGNUSSEN

GOING

BIG

LESSONS ON
SUCCESS
— in —
BUSINESS, LIFE
— and —
FAITH

A MEMOIR

This book is a beautiful blend of business wisdom and Christian faith, told through the eyes of a devout family man. It's like receiving heartfelt advice from your cherished grandfather, filled with proverbs and personal stories.

— *Pete Maddocks, Lead Teaching Pastor, Creekside Church*

Going Big is a delightful read that will inspire any up-and-coming business leader to put their faith in God first and let him take care of the rest.

— *Michael Hayhoe, Senior Investment Advisor, Mandeville Private Client Inc. and The Hayhoe Team*

Richard's story is one of hard work, incredible perseverance, and deep faith in Jesus. Powerful evidence of the difference that Jesus makes in the life of a family. Great leadership principles based on the wisdom of God's Word!.

— *Harold Albrecht, MP Kitchener-Conestoga, 2006-2019*

Through carefully weaving the stories of his life with the principles that guide his decisions, Richard Magnussen encourages all of us to "go big" when it comes to business, philanthropy, family, and faith.

— *Ryan Snider, PhD, Managing Director, Socially Responsible Safaris*

In *Going Big,* Richard Magnussen candidly shares the fascinating story of growth and global success in his family business. He reminds each of us that biblical wisdom and faith can be the foundation in all areas of life and business. His commitment to excellence and growth in every facet of life is both encouraging and inspiring.

— *Lyndon Hiebert, President, Halchemix, research-proven nutrition*

Published by Siretona Creative. www.siretona.com
978-1-998249-22-0 eBook
978-1-998249-21-3 paperback

Cover and interior design by Gary Horsman
Cover photos: Louis Venne Photography, Inc.
Interior layout: [details]

Distributed to the trade by Ingram Book Company.

DEDICATION

Marilyn, my best friend and sweetheart since she was 15 years old, has encouraged me to write this memoir.

It is an honor to dedicate this memoir to Marilyn and my six children: Kelly, Lisa, Laura Lee, Kim, Josh, and Nathan. My children, sons-in-law, and daughter-in-law have taught me so many things and have enriched my life.

TABLE OF CONTENTS

FOREWORD
by Ken Taylor

As iron sharpens iron, so a friend sharpens a friend.
~ Proverbs 27:17 NLT

I REMEMBER THE FIRST TIME I MET HIM.

A dozen of us were sitting around a large boardroom table in a windowless room. We were about ten minutes into the agenda when Richard arrived. He was late. The senior pastor playfully teased him about his tardiness. But Richard had come directly from the airport after traveling on business overseas. It spoke of his commitment to the roles he was involved in.

Richard is an imposing figure. With a 6-feet-4-inch frame and an air of confidence about him, you feel his presence in the room. I don't recall much of what we worked through at that meeting, but it was the first of hundreds of similar church leadership team meetings that he and I would participate in over a 38-year period.

I was the new Pastor of Young Adults and Outreach at First Baptist Church. It was the beginning of a special friendship with Richard that would have significant impact in sharpening my life and ministry. Richard would teach me through his words, his actions, his compassion, his integrity, his generosity, and his humility to Go Big.

I have often pondered the trajectory of my life and thanked God repeatedly that He graciously and generously gifted my wife Carol and me with special friends like Richard and Marilyn. We raised our kids together, vacationed, sailed, power boated, cried, and did a whole lot more together. Words cannot express the joy they have brought into our lives.

This book will paint a profile of Richard, but like all biographies it only provides highlights of what he has done and who he is. Please understand that this is more than a biography.

Woven throughout the fabric of the book are powerful leadership principles, parenting tips, marriage wisdom, friendship insights, and a whole lot more. Richard is not the hero in every story. And, well, that's good. None of us is. But as you read this book and get to know the man you will be touched by his life and perhaps it will nudge you to Go Big.

A big thank you to you, Richard, and to the family and team who contributed to this book. It's special and I absolutely loved reading it.

Stay in His dust,
Ken

INTRODUCTION

IT SHOULD NEVER HAVE HAPPENED.

I started small in a life that led to going big.

At the end of high school, I wanted to follow one of four paths for my career: join the RCMP, become a contractor, become an architect, or join my dad in his small business.

My father immigrated from Germany as a teenager and devoted his working life to manufacturing high quality furniture in a small shop built from a chicken coop and big dreams. I decided to follow in his steps. At age twenty I knew how to make furniture but didn't understand anything about business, let alone know the difference between sales and marketing. I should have had an MBA or at least a degree in economics or in managing people. What I did have was a managing partner, and he had big ideas in mind for us.

I was as pleasantly surprised as anyone. Magnussen Home Furniture grew to become one of the most aggressive global residential furniture companies with a good name in the industry as Canada's largest supplier serving customers worldwide, sourced by distribution centers in Vietnam and California. When my partner and I started the journey in 1970, I had no inkling of what would happen by the time I retired in 2016:

- Going from an annual revenue of $38,000 to over $200 million;
- Manufacturing 150,000 pieces of furniture a month;
- Having 300 team members managing 10,000 contracted workers globally;
- Selling furniture in over 20 countries;
- Being elected as president of the American Home Furniture Industry;
- Working with foreign governments.

Going big has been a thrilling, fulfilling, often surprising, and never dull ride of family and business success lasting over fifty years. Ride is an intentional choice of words, because in the furniture business the term "ride" refers to how comfortable a sofa or chair feels. Life was far from being a comfortable ride, but it was crafted with higher purpose.

I'm indebted to my managing partner and, while I am thankful for how God has led, I find that younger leaders, who are trying to figure things out, often ask a question that really lights me up: How can I be successful?

The question opens a door to what you will read on the following pages.

That's my challenge.

It's a good day when I can take on a challenge.

Just like the day that Marilyn and I and our pastor and his wife, went to see the apartment of a man from our church who is wheelchair bound. Pastor Ken had suggested that Steve could use some new paint for his living space. As soon as we walked in, I whispered to Ken, "This place needs more than paint."

I arranged for the manager to meet me on the street outside the apartment and after a lengthy conversation about the extent of the renovations and my wherewithal, received approval to have at it.

That's how I see things.

There's always a way.

And if there isn't a way, we'll make one.

I know I inherited that attitude from my dad. He used to say, "The impossible we do today. The miraculous will take us a little longer."

I like going big. If you're going to do something you might as well go big. My life is a long litany of innovations and finding a way through adversity:

- Using my paralyzed arm to stabilize the gurney I was on in an ambulance rushing me to a Mexican hospital where the physicians were also the maintenance workers.
- Marketing high quality imported furniture from Taiwan when anything labeled "made in Taiwan" was seen as junk.

- Operating a warehouse in Vietnam, where extreme humidity would destroy wooden furniture and making use of an unusual solution.
- Finding a way during the recession of 2008 to come back from a 40% drop in sales, and dealing with a bank that refused to re-finance us.
- Purchasing a boat for family use and starting a business importing yachts from southeast Asia.
- Purchasing a family home in Florida and learning to flip multi-million-dollar properties for a tidy profit.
- Taking on a bully trustee from a condo association to court and winning big.

Not that I take any credit for how my life has unfolded. I found a way to raise a family, build an international business, successfully execute a succession plan, and achieve my dreams by trusting God's ways that I learned from the Bible.

Now, from the start you need to know that I'm not going to get preachy. I'm not a Bible-thumper. But there are some gems of wisdom in the Bible that will help a person live a life of excellence. I've been to a few leadership conventions and seminars in my lifetime, and it was fascinating to hear experts share principles that had their roots in the book of Proverbs. The chapters in Proverbs are filled with state-of-the-art management tips that work.

I've lived my life choosing to do what works. Faith in God works for me.

Do you believe in miracles? I've had a few experiences that felt like miracles scattered through my life. Shortly after Marilyn and I were married. I broke my neck. Years later I had a chance encounter on a ski hill with my doctor. He introduced me to his wife by saying, "This is the guy I'm always talking about. He's a walking miracle. He should be paralyzed."

In the early days of our business, I needed the skills of an adept leader of manufacturing. He turned down my offer of employment, so I asked God for help. Not long after that, the man's circumstances shifted and he changed his mind, accepted my offer, and set up our company for success for years to come.

On occasion, my beliefs have led me to run counter to accepted business wisdom. In the mid-90s I took the unconventional step in the furniture industry of closing our wholesale showrooms on Sundays. I had a lot of salespeople pretty concerned about the decision. However, sales rose by 25% that year.

You might be inclined to see these as coincidences.

A speaker once said, "A coincidence is a small miracle in which God chooses to remain anonymous."

That perspective appeals to me.

One thing is true. I looked forward to working every day. I loved what I got to do. The lows and the highs. It was all part of the challenge.

I don't take the success I've enjoyed for granted. By no means has life been without humbling experiences. Setbacks and failures early on in business and family life literally brought me to my knees.

When I reflect on my life, I see how God was teaching me and moving me towards a life of humility. I am a long way from where I should be, but the older I get, the more I have come to realize the power and strength that humility can bring to life. Our three children, their families, and the people I've worked with, taught me that:

- humble leaders trust God;
- humble leaders listen to others;
- humble leaders see trials as opportunities.

Those practices helped me to get things right, not to be right.

Often over the years I would celebrate business success and personally take the credit, but after seeing my life play out, I know that Jesus is the real hero.

Steve Jobs said he wanted to make a dent in the Universe. This book was written using one of his products. It gives me pleasure to know that the homes, and I daresay the lives of millions of people, are enriched by products associated with the Magnussen brand. We manufactured quality furniture with our family in mind. But furniture is not my "dent."

Going Big was written with you in mind. Each chapter is salted with some of my favorite Proverbs. Many I have memorized. All have proven to be practical wisdom for facing life's biggest challenges.

I hope as you walk through this story you will experience a deeper understanding of a life situation, unexpected inspiration, a perspective that helps you see something freshly, or a way to face something differently. And I hope you will discover the reality and clarity of how living out faith in God will lead to a life of extraordinary wisdom, excellence, and generosity. I hope that this is my "dent."

I am a follower of Jesus Christ.

Go big.

1

WISE WORDS, HARD WORK

MY DAD, INGWER MAGNUSSEN, LEFT HIS PARENTS AND SIBLINGS in Germany and ventured to Canada via New York in 1929. He was nineteen.

Canada and the world were about to be rocked by the Great Depression. Canadians out of work offered themselves for 10 cents an hour, but Dad was one of the fortunate ones. His skill as a furniture maker earned him 35 cents an hour, working twelve hours a day for five days and five hours on Saturday. He liked to say the $22.75 a week was all his because income tax didn't exist. My dad was a workhorse, putting in twelve-hour workdays his entire adult life.

Wise words bring many benefits, and hard work brings rewards.
— Proverbs 12:14 (NIV)

He got his start with Globe Furniture in Kitchen-Waterloo and then moved on to Hentschel Furniture, owned by a former employee of Globe Furniture. It wasn't long before Mr. Hentschel struggled with profitability and owed my dad a couple of months' worth of income. In 1931, Dad settled his account and left Hentschel thinking, *I can do better myself.* That decision led him to a 50' x 14' chicken coop, which he purchased for $20.00 to house his new business, Magnussen Furniture.

Dad built chesterfield frames. He was a perfectionist and proud of it. And a savvy businessman. He quickly turned a good profit, enabling him to purchase a planer, a spindle shaper, a bandsaw, sander, and saws for his work. It wasn't long before he outgrew the place and rented 1600 square feet of space from the Public Utilities. In less than twenty-four months he bought two lots for $80 and drew up building plans for a two-story, 40' x 50' building. He paid $5 for a building permit.

His company produced 1,000 tables and magazine racks at a time. The racks sold for $1.00 each and the tables for $1.50. As the years went by, he built bigger tables that sold for $20.00 each. His biggest customer for the magazine racks and tables was Conklin Shows, the largest travelling midway company in North America.

Good planning and hard work lead to prosperity."
— Proverbs 21:5 (NIV)

In 1940, World War Two broke out. In 1942, he met my mother, Esther Ingold. On the 25th of September 1943, they married. Dad was building a new, two-story house, but it wasn't finished, so they had to move into the factory office where he had lived as a bachelor. Mom endured that for a year and half and was relieved when they finally moved into their brand-new, spacious home in the spring of 1944. At the same time, Dad was drafted into the Canadian Army and served for about five months.

My sister Alice was born in 1947, and I came along in 1950. The house Dad built was home to most of our childhood memories. Decades later I noticed our old house was up for sale. My sister and I went and toured it. I couldn't believe how small my bedroom was. The living room was much smaller than what I remembered. What had become of our spacious home? My experience had enlarged my perspective and shrank my memories. We all live in bigger homes than we did back in the 50s and that house was built in the 40s.

From as early as I can remember, Alice and I worked in Dad's shop. Our family esteemed a rigorous work ethic. We lived close enough that when our school day was finished, we could walk over to the shop and start to work. I swept the floors. Dad insisted I do my work meticulously. Alice hated going to the shop because she had a strong reaction to dust. Allergies weren't something that people talked about at the time and not much was known about them. Her job was to push wood through the sanding machine and fold newspapers for packing the furniture. She would open the newspaper to the center page so the packers could use single sheets to pack the furniture. We got two cents a pound to take newspapers and open them flat to single sheets.

When we were teens, some of Alice's friends wanted to earn extra spending money so Dad hired them to help. As I remember, Dad was always safety-conscious, especially with young people working in the factory.

Our mother loved Christmas. She looked forward to Alice helping her decorate the Christmas tree with icicles and ornaments. I wasn't into decorating, but I did love my mother's baking. Every Christmas she would make her specialty: fruit cake and cookies. On Christmas Eve we would open gifts painfully slowly, one gift at a time. Christmas morning, we would sit at the kitchen table, Dad read the story of Jesus' birth from the Bible, we played board games and ate nuts and chocolate.

My mother was a Pentecostal Christian. Her life changed when she realized she could have a personal relationship with Jesus. My dad was Lutheran. They got married in a United Church and settled on attending First Baptist Church in Waterloo. My dad didn't prefer the charismatic side of Pentecostal and Mom didn't like the staleness of Lutherans. First Baptist would have been a little bit of a stretch for my dad. He was European, a glass of wine was no big deal to him, but that was a struggle at First Baptist. So, he gave it up. He couldn't see the biblical perspective against drinking wine, but he wanted to cooperate. He wasn't a rebel. He had faith in Jesus. He just had a little trouble with some of the rules, so he stayed quiet about his differences.

Our church was a Bible-believing church that offered a program called Bible Busy Bees for kids like me. We heard stories from the Bible about Noah, Moses, Goliath, Jesus and the disciples, made crafts, sang songs, and played games. One story I heard over and over was about sin. For a little kid that was serious stuff. I wasn't exactly sure what sin was, but I knew it was something bad and God didn't like it. Everyone had sin, including me, and we needed to ask Jesus for forgiveness.

I think I had an overly sensitive conscience. That was never more evident than when I started smoking.

I was four or five, old enough that my mother trusted me to be out on the sidewalk, but not so old that I was going anywhere. One afternoon I noticed a cigarette butt on the street. It was the kind of thing that would catch the attention of a curious kid. So, I picked it up, put it between my lips, and smoked it. I can just imagine a parent saying, "Oh my goodness, your child picking up a cigarette that someone else had smoked!" There wasn't much to my smoking, but did I ever feel instant guilt. That little incident made me feel I was not following what Jesus would want for me. All I knew was I needed to get in line with what Jesus wanted. And that's when I felt compelled to confess. I was anxious about how Jesus and my mother would react.

I arrived home in my state of guilt and thought my mother could see right through me and understand what a terrible sinner I was. I don't remember what I told my mother, but the next thing I knew we were on our knees by our big, old, stuffed, wine-colored couch that was probably in style at the time. My mother led me to repeat a prayer asking God to forgive my sin and for Jesus to come into my life as my Savior. When I said, "Amen," my mom looked pleased.

Mom planted a thought in my mind that stayed with me all my life. Follow Jesus. Rather than giving me a list of rules about what not to do, she gave me one thing. Love Jesus. Do things that Jesus would love. "Richard, take care of your walk with God. Jesus is always with you."

My son, keep your father's command and do not forsake your mother's teaching. Bind them always on your heart, fasten them around your neck. When you walk, they will guide you; when you sleep, they will watch over you; when you awake, they will speak to you.
— Proverbs 6:20-22 (NIV)

It was natural for us to go to church every Sunday. In my formative years, and in my teenage and young adult years, the only church I ever knew was First Baptist. It wasn't a perfect church, as none are, but it was one that helped me know God. At age 14, I was baptized in water as a follower of Jesus. We practiced full immersion at our church. I was given a blue gown to wear over my swimsuit. I went down the steps into the baptism tank and the gown floated in the water like a life jacket. I was baptized just like the original disciples were, only they were in a river.

I was very active in the young people's group and a program for boys called Christian Service Brigade. Becoming a Brigade leader was the first of many such roles in my lifetime. That responsibility was the beginning of learning how churches work.

The Christian Service Brigade was asked to supply the ushers at church once a year. When I was 18, I was made responsible for organizing the ushers on that Sunday. One of the Brigade members was about 15 years old. He was a "Herald of Christ," which is the top level in Brigades, kind of like an Eagle Scout. He had to do a lot of work to get the award. However, when it came to ushering, he had a fault. His hair was touching his ears. That was a big no-no back then, even though I had no idea why.

I was asked by the man in charge of ushering to remove this young guy from the volunteers because of his hair. That's when I learned one of my first lessons in leadership. I respected leadership, so I did what I was asked to do. But I did march in to see the senior pastor afterwards. He oversaw all the programs, so I thought I might as well go to the top and get it straightened out. I tried to act respectfully. I asked him, "I don't get this. I'm sure Jesus had hair touching his ears. As a Nazarite he wouldn't have cut his hair." And so on. Anyways, the pastor agreed with me. The kid still couldn't usher but I felt like I was in the right.

Unfortunately, the pastor agreed with everyone. I could go in, and he would agree with me and then he would agree with the guy who was driving the legalism. There was an attitude of legalism—rules that didn't come from the Bible but were a big deal in the church. My dad struggled with that as well. Must be a Magnussen thing. But that didn't throw me off church. It challenged me to manage conflict well and be gracious, but also to question why things were done as they were. It's easy to get off track on some of those religious rules. I'm grateful to First Baptist Church because I was given the opportunity to learn leadership and to be a part of working through the Holy Spirit to adjust and make changes.

School was a different issue. There were no gold stars on my assignments in public school. I never did well in grammar and spelling. When it was time for high school I was put in a slow learners' class. The students in that class would take two years of grades 9 and 10 and then go to work in a factory or learn a trade. When my Grade 9 year started, I realized this was not the class for me. I wanted to learn technical things about the trades but that's not all I cared about.

I went to the guidance counsellor and said, "I don't really want to be in this class. I want to be with the regular students." I was respectful in what I said. The counsellor said, "That's really a big leap to go from where you are to that level. Stay in the class for a year and we'll see how you do." Long story short,

I got 90s in the course, and they said, "We'll give you a shot in the regular course" and I got 85%. The difference was that I was now serious. Maybe I had been bored. I should have paid more attention. But when I decided that I wanted to work hard, I did well.

I started my career with no business degree, only Grade 12. I enrolled at Conestoga College in Kitchener in a four-year Construction Technology program but did not return after my first year. I still loved business, but college wasn't for me. I wanted to be a builder, or an architect, or work in a small shop. And I thought, *You know what, I'll try working in my dad's little shop and if it's too boring, we'll figure it out later.* One theory I had was that it's easier to steer a car that's rolling than it is to try and direct it when it's stopped.

Marilyn and I advocate for kids to get a post-secondary education, although I think everybody's pushing them to become accountants or lawyers. There's so much in the trades that people could really do well at, and some people are more inclined for a trade.

The basics of business came from learning the business from my dad. I never had any formal woodworking training, just from him. But I was teachable. I like learning. I read magazines about business, and I would talk with people and always ask questions. My dad was great at asking questions and I learned that from him. Connie Lineberry was one of those people who answered my questions. She worked for *Furniture Today* in sales and advertising and worked with me on industry ads in their weekly newspaper for the industry. At one time, I explained to her that I didn't understand the difference between marketing and sales. That seems so funny to me now. She said, "Well, I've never been asked that question, especially from a CEO." I got my degree in business the hard way, much like how I learned most everything important in my life.

To acquire wisdom is to love yourself; people who cherish understanding will prosper.
— Proverbs 19:8 (NLT)

My dad had a complex personality. He was very hard to work with, but he was the life of the party. Generally, people liked him, but they didn't like to work for him because he was a perfectionist. That's why he had a hard time keeping employees. It wasn't that they didn't like him at work, but he was a hard man to please. I could be very compliant. My dad said I had to work, and I worked. There was no sleeping in on Saturdays. In high school, I was tall for my age and the basketball coach wanted me on his team. But my dad said, "Oh no, no. You will come to the factory after school, and I have work for you. I need you here. You won't be playing basketball after school, and I need you to be working Saturdays." When he wanted the lawn cut and the gardens weeded, I didn't resist.

I couldn't fault my dad for being a hard worker. He was a bear for punishment when it came to his entrepreneurial work ethic. Dad toiled 16-hours a day for years. Mother would often say he was working too hard but that didn't deter him. When I became the one responsible for the business, I understood exactly why he did what he did.

Dad taught me the value of a dollar. He took me to the bank when I wasn't tall enough to look over the counter. I would push the 25 cents I earned from doing chores across the counter to the bank teller and she would record it in my account book. Watching my account grow was a good feeling but it seemed to take forever to reach my goals. My friends would get $5.00 in allowance for doing nothing, but I had to work for my 25 cents. When I wanted to buy a bicycle, my dad said he would pay half for it. I wondered why he was so hard on me. Really, he was doing me a favor by helping me realize and appreciate the value of a dollar.

A little extra sleep, a little more slumber, a little folding of the hands to rest—then poverty will pounce on you like a bandit; scarcity will attack you like an armed robber.
— Proverbs 24:33-34 (NLT)

When I was eight or nine, I learned that families aren't perfect, even those who go to church. My mom and dad used to get sideways once in a while. At times in the evenings, after my sister and I had gone to bed, we heard them arguing very loudly downstairs. Alice and I would get out of our beds and sit at the top of the second story stairway. She would try to comfort me because I was upset over their arguing. I won't use the word fighting because there was no physical abuse. But their bickering bothered me. When I think about my childhood, that is the closest I came to experiencing trauma. In some ways it either shaped or simply reflected how I was wired. I would go downstairs and try to be the peacemaker. That is typical of my behavior all through life, at home and in business. Years later when we toured our old house, I saw the very steps we sat on and all the feelings came back to me.

For all their love for me and my sister, Mom and Dad had a struggling relationship. That was very difficult for me as a child. It made me feel insecure, dreading that one of my parents was going to leave. Back then, families splitting up wasn't common. Maybe in society it was more common than I realized, but not at First Baptist Church.

There were other signs that everything wasn't perfect. Whenever my parents and I would go on a walk, my dad would walk ahead. If we were going up a hill, I would wait and take my mom by the hand to make sure she was fine. I don't know where that came from. I wouldn't have learned it from my dad. I was told that he was a fun guy at parties but not so much at home. As a child I wanted to get my parents to argue less. All my life my mother and sister told me that I got my drive from my dad and my sensitivity from my mother. My dad was the visionary. Mom was the homemaker who kissed and hugged hurts away.

There's one other drama from my early years. An uncle dealt with mental illness. He was in a London, Ontario hospital. My parents would go and visit him, and they would take Alice and me. We had to sit on these hard little benches and my parents would go in behind the bars. That was a far cry from how people are treated today, but that was then. Some of the patients would come up to where we were sitting. They weren't dangerous, but they seemed strange to us as kids. They would put their faces very close to my face and want to know who I was. I felt terrified. I don't think my parents realized what was happening.

My uncle was schizophrenic. He went off his medication and ended up freezing to death in a little backyard shed. Some neighborhood boys found him. He must have thought somebody was chasing him.

At church there were some adults with special needs. When they would come close to talk with Marilyn and me, she observed that I would back up two or three steps. One time we visited a home where there were people with special needs. Marilyn noticed that I would take a step back every time anyone came face-to-face with me. "You're afraid."

I said, "I'm not afraid. I'm six foot four. What would I be afraid of?"

"You wouldn't have anything to be afraid of, but you're afraid and that's from your childhood."

I didn't realize it then, but a pattern was forming that would play out over the course of our marriage. "You know what? I hate to admit it, but you're right."

Fortunately for me, Marilyn had a clear perspective on my childhood. Her wise words forecast some hard work that I would face in the future.

Chapter 1, Wise Words, Hard Work

Although I was raised with a good work ethic, I performed below my academic potential prior to Grade 9. I wasn't motivated until I saw where my behavior was taking me. One of Stephen Covey's habits of highly successful people is, "Begin with the end in mind."

- What end do you have in mind?
- Reflecting on your childhood experiences, what is the earliest childhood crisis that you remember?
- When you mull over your childhood crisis and other past experiences, what comes to mind about how they affect your present behavior patterns and attitudes?
- Are you who you want to be right now? What do you have to say about yourself?
- How do you want to be remembered?

2

MARRIAGE IS WHAT YOU MAKE IT

IT SEEMED LIKE MARILYN MCGOEY AND I HAD KNOWN EACH other all our lives.

From the time we were little kids in the same church and Sunday School classes, our paths often crossed. But we really didn't become familiar with each other until we were teenagers and in youth group. Marilyn was 15 when we started dating. She says what she loved most was my ability to always find something humorous in any situation. That is interesting. I'm not given to laughter. I like making people laugh, but I'm not inclined to laugh out loud. Our family teases me about this. Marilyn's family will howl with laughter, and I'll sit quietly with a smile on my face—the extent of my laughter.

Marilyn says she was attracted to my work ethic, so that didn't work out badly after all.

I'm not very romantic but I worked at it with Marilyn. I tried to notice things that she appreciated and made sure that I got them for her on occasion. But I think I won her heart by being in the kitchen. I was very comfortable making a meal and took even more pleasure in plating the meal. Presentation was the key, and I would go to great lengths to make the meal look even better than it tasted.

Our first official date was a sign of things to come. I didn't drive. When I went to her house to pick her up, we had to take the city bus to see my best friend David play hockey. He was the Captain of the Kitchener Rangers OHA team and headed for the NHL. After the game we caught a bus back to her place. As I was about to say good night, I told Marilyn that I didn't like taking the bus while on a date.

I explained that this would be our last date until I got my license.

She replied matter-of-factly. "OK."

Six months later, on my birthday, I got my license.

It was summertime. The first thing I did was phone her and say, "I got my license and I'd like to make a date for this Saturday."

Marilyn responded, "I can't. I'm not available this Saturday. I will be going out with my future brother-in-law's brother."

When I heard that I decided to ask out her best friend, Karen Bauer. That did not sit very well with Marilyn. But it wasn't like we were going steady, as we called it back then.

There was another time when she couldn't go out with me, so I asked her cousin on a date. Did I do that to bug her? Marilyn thought so. I knew her hot button and was quite willing to frequently press it. But that was just my Magnussen sense of humor. And history shows that we somehow survived it.

I was at that stage where I needed to figure life out. When I was 17 or 18, I had a brief flirtation with joining the RCMP, much to my father's chagrin.

Marilyn's uncle was an RCMP officer who served in the Northwest Territories, got promoted to a higher rank and was training new recruits in Saskatchewan. A career with the RCMP seemed intriguing to me. I'm certain I would have qualified for the Force, because in those days they wanted height and my six-foot four frame would have been appealing, even if my friends did call me "string bean." I went as far as getting an application, but when I realized that training would take me to Saskatoon and away from Marilyn, I had a sober second thought. In all likelihood, I may never have returned to Ontario if I joined the Force because the RCMP was on the federal level and Ontario had the Ontario Provincial Police force (OPP). I decided not to pursue a career in law enforcement.

Contractor or architect were considerations, but when Dad said to me, "I'm not pushing you into the furniture business, because you've got to love it, but I do want to retire," I reasoned that this could be my opportunity. The building was paid for. The machinery was paid for. We had no debt. I thought the job would probably be boring, but I said I'd like to give it a shot. In 1970, at the age of 20, I started working full-time with my dad. I haven't found that boring day yet.

We were the definition of a small business: a couple of part-time people in a small manufacturing shop, some high school students in production, and a few local customers. Our annual sales were $38,000. My father had trained me from the age of ten to sweep floors, make the furniture and apply finishes. Three months after I started, Dad announced that he was going to visit relatives in Germany, handed me a list of suppliers and contacts, and said "You're in charge, Richard. See you in six weeks." Dad never said anything later about that being his strategy to draw my heart into the business, but it worked. I love challenges.

My first and biggest challenge was to engage more customers. Fortunately, engaging customers proved to be less of a challenge than getting engaged to Marilyn.

Our engagement was something to remember. I was 20 and Marilyn was 19. We had looked at rings and talked about our future. When I was ready to pop the question, I told Marilyn we'd be going to Toronto for a meal. And going into Toronto from Kitchener for a meal was a big deal back in the 70s. My parents loaned me their little red Volkswagen. The ring was burning a hole in my pocket when I went to pick her up, so I put it in the glove compartment. We headed for Toronto, and I couldn't get my mind off the ring. After a few minutes of driving, I couldn't wait any longer and asked Marilyn to open the glove compartment. There was a box. I asked her to open it and at the next red light I asked her to marry me. Marilyn reminds me that she found that to be cute and romantic in itself, even though it wasn't the most romantic place. It wasn't the way she would have wanted it, but she said yes!

I'd planned to impress Marilyn at a fancy restaurant down by Lake Ontario. There was a bit of a waiting line. We got up to the maître d' and I said "There's a reservation for two people under the name Richard Magnussen."

And he said, "Sir, you do not have a jacket on. You cannot enter the restaurant without a jacket."

I asked if he had one that I could wear.

"No, I don't."

I said, "I'd like to talk to the manager."

And the manager came along and said, "I'm sorry, sir, you cannot enter without a jacket."

What do you do now? There were other restaurants around, but when we tried a few they were all full. We got back in the car, headed back along Lakeshore Drive, and finally came across a restaurant in a hotel. I don't remember the name of the hotel, but I can't forget the older lady that was on a platform playing an organ to entertain the diners. It was hilarious. That's a lesson on how not to do an engagement dinner.

I married a firecracker.

Marilyn is of Irish descent on her dad's side. She's fiery and when she gets fired up at me, I just say, "That spice is why I married you." Brings the temperature right down and I really mean it. I do like that she speaks her mind.

Marilyn and I came from completely opposite kinds of families, which upped the complexity factor in our first year of marriage. Both families were very traditional, but that's where the similarities ended. Marilyn's father was far more engaged in helping at home. My father was absolutely not. My father came home from work at whatever time he wanted and that was totally acceptable in our household. But it wasn't in Marilyn's. My erratic arrival times from work did not go over real well. A set dinnertime was important. When the food was ready, I should be home. And if I was going to be late, she reminded me that the phone does work.

We had to learn to work through a lot of things. Marilyn and I spent a few summer weekends in our first year of marriage at my parents' cottage. Spending time together was a way for Marilyn to get to know my family better. On the drive home following one weekend get-together, she explained she had some concerns. The bickering I experienced as a child was still a part of my parents' behavior. I had become deaf to it, but it was on high volume for Marilyn. She didn't feel comfortable where there were ongoing quarrels over petty things. That behavior wasn't in her family, and she didn't want it in our family. It was a tough pill for me to swallow, but I understood that Marilyn wanted to safeguard the culture of our family. We agreed it wouldn't be acceptable to have any kind of disagreement or to speak critically about each other in front of the kids. Not that we wanted to hide anything, but we wanted our kids to hear us talking each other up, not putting each other down. That one choice may have saved us a lot of future grief.

Money was tight, like it is for most young couples. Marilyn made her dresses and clothes for the kids. She was exceptional at managing our household on a tight budget. When we purchased something, it was paid for before we bought it. We saved up and didn't buy anything on credit.

I was a very busy guy. She was the glue that kept our little family together. Business was growing by leaps and bounds. I was involved on the Deacon board at church and on a few other boards. All too often, Marilyn was home, alone with the kids.

We invested in our marriage by attending weekend marriage conferences, including one with Gary Smalley. He was funny. Gary tells a story about their family dog whose bark was creating problems, so he bought one of those collars with a metal piece that would deliver a small shock when the dog barked. While Gary was sleeping in his recliner, his sons put the collar on him and then provoked the dog to bark. Gary jumped up and ran out the door, leaving his boys rolling on the floor.

I felt some small shocks more than once at those conferences. Who knew that women and men hold different perspectives on things, like shopping? If Marilyn and I were to go shopping for a blue blouse for her, right away I'd find three options in her size because I wanted to make the purchase and get out of the store ASAP. She has a whole different agenda. It frustrated me that she would look around, take her time, enjoy the moment. "Do I want this blue or that shade of blue? How does it look on me? Maybe there is a prettier one in a different store. Aren't we having fun?" It's the experience that matters to her as much as the purchase.

I was a slob.

I thought nothing of leaving my clothes on the bedroom floor. That was never an issue for my mother. Who knew a wife would be different? But Marilyn had a solution: she would kick my clothes into the closet and shut the door. And that was that. She refused to pick up after me.

I told her, "Let's make a deal. You like to hang up your clothes at the end of the day. I like to leave my clothes on a chair when I go to bed. However, I'll always have my clothes picked up by the next morning. When the bed's made and the room's cleaned up, then the clothes will be picked up." Deal.

Now having said that, did Marilyn ever pick up my clothes? Yes. On occasion. And you know what? Sometimes she still does. And can you imagine what she says to herself? "When you pick something up, just say, at least I have a husband that I can pick up after, so let's not complain about it."

No wonder I love her.

Here's another one. We're out driving and there's a narrow space and I know I can get through it with a Mack truck, and she thinks I'm going to crash. I didn't know that there is a difference between the peripheral visions of men and women. It was good for us to discover some of these things together. "Oh, that's why you do what you do" or "That's why you're the way you are." "Calm down, Richard." We couldn't get enough of the content, so we purchased a whole series of marriage talks on eight-track tapes.

I'm the visionary. Marilyn is the organizer. She keeps me grounded. I invested in property on Georgian Bay to build a cottage. My plan was to build as soon as I got the land. Marilyn thought we should wait because of the kids' stage of life. We waited ten years to build. But she was right. I've told her when I have one of these visions now, my shelf life is too short to wait ten years.

I'll go into our washroom and there's a sticky note on the mirror. That's Marilyn. She left it as a reminder that it was somebody's birthday or there was a dinner meeting with friends. She keeps track of all the grandkids' birthdays and our children's wedding anniversaries and helps me look like a hero when I call them to celebrate. She knows I need reminders. Birthdays and anniversaries weren't a big deal growing up in my family. They were in hers.

A good woman is hard to find, and worth far more than diamonds.
— Proverbs 31:10 (MSG)

Marilyn was such a big support in those early years of our business. She was the deciding factor in making our marriage work while I was working on the business. Marriage is not a 50/50 partnership. It's 100/100. A business owner can be a success in marriage with a partner willing to make life work.

Chapter 2, Marriage Is What You Make It

Gary Smalley, psychologist and family coach, says, "Life is relationships, the rest is just details." Think about your relationships. I entered marriage not knowing I needed to learn a lot as a husband.

- Are you bringing your best to your primary relationships?
- Do those closest to you love and respect you the most?
- Everyone needs a mentor, someone who sees their potential. Who are your mentors? What are you learning from them?

3

GROWING PAINS

THE BEST THINGS THAT EVER HAPPENED TO ME ARE NAMED Kelly, Lisa, and Laura.

Marilyn and I were married not quite a year when she became pregnant. We wanted children, even though Marilyn was only 20. She was ecstatic. I was a little nervous. A lot nervous. Responsibility was setting in for this young fellow taking on a business and a wife and now a family.

We were living in a small, one-bedroom apartment. Marilyn wanted to buy a house, but I wasn't ready. Imagine that. So, we moved into a two-bedroom apartment in the same building. Marilyn loved it. She made drapes, we moved in furniture that my parents had stored, painted the walls, bought a new mattress, and put wallpaper up. It was a fun, exciting time. Marilyn quit work about three months after she found out she was pregnant, so she had lots of time to do things that she loved and, in her words, "fluff the nest." She does that well.

Naming your firstborn is a big deal. We thought about Jason, but everyone was naming their sons Jason. There was a student working for us, a good kid who worked hard, and his name was Kelly. I asked Marilyn what she thought of that name for a boy. Both of us quite liked it.

Kelly was supposed to arrive on the 25th of September, but he wasn't born until the 27th of October. There was a miscalculation in the dates and by this time Marilyn had lost her patience. It was her birthday, so she phoned her doctor and said, "It's my 21st birthday. Could you not do something for me to-day?" The doctor said, "Meet me at the hospital tomorrow and we'll get things going." She was induced and Kelly was born around 8:00 that night. Marilyn did very well. Me, not so much.

Against my initial reluctance, I was with her in the delivery room. In those days, you had to take a course if you wanted to be in for the delivery. My story was I was busy working so I never took the course. Marilyn says I was skittish and didn't want anything to do with a delivery room. In 1972 it wasn't common for husbands to be in delivery rooms. She was going to have to go it alone.

But I surprised her. I drove her to the hospital and said to the doctor, "I really want to be in there."

Our doctor, Margaret Austrup, asked, "Well, do you faint?"

And I said, "No, I don't think so. I'll be good."

She said, "Well, we can't look after you if you faint. She's our first priority, then the baby, so we'll just leave you on the floor."

And of course, that was a big deal to get admitted without taking the course. She took favor on me, and I was there for the whole birth. And that was amazing. I had to wear a gown and gloves and mask up. And for the record, I didn't faint.

When Kelly was due, I was finishing and spraying furniture. We had a quality inspector named Mabel Schmidt. She had one eye, but she could see better than people with two eyes. She never missed anything. She told me, "Richard, you had a lot of runs in your spray job. A lot of this product has to be re-sanded and recoated." Apparently, the day before Marilyn went in for the birth, my quality was way down. I guess the anticipation of becoming a first-time father did get to me.

I bought a new suit to go and pick Marilyn up when she was discharged. Kelly was a beautiful child. His grandparents were enthralled with him. We never had an issue finding someone to sit with him so we could have a break. He started to walk fairly early, and he was a tease. We would hold our arms out and he would come towards us. Then he'd laugh and turn away from us. He would bolt left or right, laughing, and then we'd grab him and he would laugh all the more. To this day he is a teaser.

Our son's full given name was Kelly Maurice Magnussen. Maurice was my grandfather's name. Kelly never liked his middle name. At school, he had to give his full name and he was embarrassed by it. We gave him that middle name to honor my parents, but Kelly never met my grandfather, so the name held no significance to him. When he was ten, he asked to change his name. We said, "Well, what would you like?"

"I want Richard. I want Dad's name."

So, we went to a lawyer and that's why he is Kelly Richard Magnussen.

When Marilyn became pregnant with our second child, she thought it was time to buy a house. She was right, but I was scared to death to buy a house. I know that sounds hard to believe, especially coming from a businessman, but I was reluctant to add more debt to an already high load. Still, Marilyn was determined we were getting a house and rightly so. The little I knew about real estate was you buy location, and you make your profit on the purchase.

I found a house with some upside in a desirable neighborhood and showed it to Marilyn. She didn't like my choice. "Why does it have to be in this neighborhood?"

I said, "Because I think a return on the investment will be better in this neighborhood."

Marilyn liked the smaller neighborhood. I was go big. Real estate is location, location, location. It was the first house on Academy Crescent. Not a great house but one that had potential. A split-level, close to the University, so we could rent it to students and have them live in the lower level without affecting our lives. She didn't love it, but she bought in. The mortgage was going to be $300 a month. That seemed like a lot back in the early 70s. But when we offered the downstairs for rent, two students applied immediately and gave us $150 each for rent. So they were paying the mortgage and I'm thinking, *OK, that's better.* We bought the house for $55,000 and sold it for $107,000 eight years later. It was a good lesson on return on investment and buying in a good location.

I was adjusting to our new marriage and my new business responsibilities. I had big dreams that stretched beyond our little shop in Waterloo. I knew I needed to get furniture sales, but I'd never learned anything about sales. The furniture orders my father took were all he made. He had two salesmen working for him, but I knew I needed to get out and learn sales. And what better way to do it than to go where it was done?

I packed a bag lunch, a book with store addresses so I knew where the retailers were located, a map to find them, and then I'd go to Toronto for the day. I told myself, "You're not coming home until you have paid for your trip." I spent my time on King and Queen streets where there were a lot of Mom-and-Pop furniture stores.

One day I got up enough nerve to go in and meet the Leons. Today, most Canadians have heard of Leon's, one of Canada's most highly respected furniture retailers. However, in 1970 they operated only five stores and were as much about appliances as they were about furniture. By national standards, they were quite small, but five stores were a big deal to me. Leon's had a reputation as an honest, reputable retailer who provided quality merchandise at low prices.

I ventured in and met Ed Leon. He was smoking a big stogie cigar. In those days you could smoke in an office. He sat behind an elevated desk because he was a shorter guy. I'm tall so I sat on a chair below, which levelled out our playing field. I kind of smiled about it. For some reason he took a liking to me and fired off a lot of questions. He wanted to know what was making me tick.

I realized afterwards he wasn't really interested in my furniture offering, but my potential. I think he saw somebody who had a lot of drive, wanted to learn and could be good for his business. He certainly wasn't into charity for me, that's for sure. The outcome he wanted was to have some tables to match upholstery and if he could influence the way the design was made, it would be a win for him. The only thing I offered Leon's was a can-do attitude, passion about making furniture, a willingness to listen, and the commitment to produce what the customer wanted at a low cost.

Ed Leon taught me everything I needed to know about sales. He gave me some great advice: "Make sure your door is open to anybody. You never know who is going to help you grow your business." That advice motivated me to attend furniture trade shows, where I met sales representatives who picked up Magnussen's line of tables, allowing our company to penetrate the Canadian market outside Ontario.

Getting wisdom is the wisest thing you can do! and whatever else you do, develop good judgment.
— Proverbs 4:7 (NLT)

Years later, as our company expanded internationally, "keeping the door open to anybody" meant I refused to relinquish the small independent stores that I started with. I had an experience with a supplier who declined to sell to me because my company wasn't big enough, and the memory of that door being closed on me has remained ever since. I believed that any customer may become a big customer someday, and if he doesn't, he's still a good customer.

The Grossman brothers were owners of a company called Artistic Furniture. Ben Grossman leased a show room at the Toronto International, a major Canadian furniture show held in January and June. Ed Leon was a customer and visited Ben's show room. He saw potential, so he introduced me to the Grossmans. Ben saw what I could do. He wanted me to make tables that matched his upholstery. That was big. Consumers could purchase a whole living room of matching sofa, armchair, end tables, and coffee table or a bedroom package of furniture. This was the pioneer early stages of package deals, which became a hit.

Ben was a really tough Jewish guy, but I liked him a lot and I knew he liked me because he was rough on me. He treated me like a son. Whenever I made a mistake, he'd hit me over the back of the head. Not physically, but he'd tell me why I shouldn't do that. He taught me sales in his showroom. With his coaching, I employed a whole group of sales agents that wanted to sell tables that would match the upholstery.

And that's how Magnussen started growing. It wouldn't have been the same if I was by myself in the showroom compared to having the influence of a manufacturer that was doing well with the big guys and small guys.

Ed taught me the value of occasional tables, coffee tables, and end tables in relationship to the sofa. "Richard," he said. "Keep your eye on what is going on in upholstery." I learned the lead sale is always upholstery. A wife will say to her husband, "We need a new sofa." She will go in for the sofa, but if it's a good store they'll close the sale on new end tables and a coffee table. The sofa looks nice matched with the tables and the salesperson can throw a new rug in to sweeten the deal. I learned to make it easy for the retailer to match something that goes with the upholstery in general.

A discerning customer will buy a coffee table that doesn't match the end table, but it matches in a bigger sense because it's the whole room appeal. The upholstery sells first. If you're not selling something that can tie into upholstery, you're barking up the wrong tree. I wanted to make furniture that was going with the trends of upholstery, so I would go to the US markets to learn what trends were on the rise.

Ed Leon inspired me to be innovative. About two years after I met him, he opened the first warehouse showroom in Canada. His massive 150,000-square foot building was the first example of "big box" retailing in the country. For the first time ever, customers had access to a multi-million-dollar inventory that prevented long delays in obtaining their purchase. Some of my "go big" thinking no doubt rubbed off from Ed.

I always held Ed in high regard. His daughter Diane started to move into the role of purchasing as they grew, so after a while I didn't get to see as much of Ed. I went to work with Diane, and she was a very talented buyer. And from there we went to her cousin Michael Leon as a buyer. The Leons had huge families. Everybody thought they were Jewish because of their really nice, tanned skin, but they were Arab Christians of Lebanese descent. They had a crucifix prominently displayed in their lobby. And every time they had a store opening, they had a priest bless the store. It was evident that Christian ideals such as kindness, humility, and a general concern for others were deeply ingrained in the Leon family.

They were tough buyers, fair but very tough.

What I picked up from Ed was instrumental years later in my negotiations in Asia. I needed all he taught me about selling to tough buyers.

Intelligent people are always ready to learn. Their ears are open for knowledge.
— Proverbs 18:15 (NLT)

I was just a high school graduate basically trying to learn from anyone willing to answer my questions. I didn't have what comes with an MBA. However, we were doubling, tripling, and quadrupling our business very quickly. The Kitchener-Waterloo Record business editor, Henry Koch, tracked me down, and published articles periodically about our growth at Magnussen Furniture. Koch was interested in the business, but more than that he was most intrigued with my faith in God. After all, faith and business can't work together, can they? I filled a file folder of his newspaper articles and others about our business success and a faith that worked.

In an article from 1975, Koch noted that while Magnussen Furniture was virtually unknown in the Kitchener/Waterloo area, our products were highly accepted across Canada and the Northwest Territories. People must feel that anything that comes 3000 miles has to be a better product, so we were selling far more tables in Victoria, BC and Newfoundland than we did in our own backyard.

The business continued to grow faster than I could believe. I was getting up at 6 AM and working fourteen-hour days, six days a week to try and keep up. It was insane. Selling, building, training, managing, hiring. I was in way over my head. Expectations were rising and my mental health was declining. Our family was growing and so was the weight on my shoulders. Relentless pressure brought me close to a breaking point.

One night, alone in the factory, I was overwhelmed. The feeling was foreign to me. Not that I was arrogant, but I had taken everything in my life in stride. Get married. Lead the business with my dad. Become a dad. Grow sales for the business. Purchase our first house. Manage personnel and the challenges that come with a growing organization. In and of themselves each challenge was manageable, but all of them at once was too much. That night I knelt down on the gritty shop floor of our little factory. It seemed like the best thing I could do when I didn't know what to do. I simply said to God, "Lord, I can't do this. I need your wisdom in this business and in all my decisions. This business is yours. You be the boss. Show me what to do." I sincerely meant what I prayed.

When I got back to my feet, I didn't feel like anything had changed. All the problems did not magically disappear. I can't say I heard God speak back to me words of reassurance. However, I soon discovered that everything was changing. I slept well that night. That was five decades ago and turning the business over to God was the wisest decision I ever made.

Choose my instruction rather than silver; and knowledge rather than pure gold.
— Proverbs 8:10 (NLT)

One of the first areas God began to instruct me in was not in the business but in my personal life. I held the idea that once I made a lot of money, then I could start being generous and giving more. God made it clear that's not the way generosity works. One of the practices Marilyn and I learned growing up was to give ten percent of what we earned back to God through our church. It was called tithing, which means, ten percent. Ever since we were little kids giving our five cents in Sunday School, we practiced giving faithfully. The first ten percent of our monthly earnings went to our church, and we felt good about that. Our idea was that giving more than ten percent was something that could wait for later when we had more money and less financial pressure. God had a different perspective on the matter.

We were setting money aside to furnish our first house with new furniture. There was about $5,000 in our savings account, which in the early 70s was a lot of money. One Sunday morning we were at church as usual but that day there was a guest speaker. A missionary who worked in Africa talked quite passionately and persuasively about the humanitarian needs in his area. At the end of his talk, he asked people to give to support the work. I remember distinctly the impression that I should give the $5,000 of our savings.

In my mind that morning I could see the spot on the shop floor with me turning the business over to God and now God wanted all the money we had saved to buy furniture. Marilyn was pregnant. I was working as hard as I could to make money, be responsible, and save. I started to sweat. That was a lot of money. Was this really God? Why would God ask us for all of our money? There were other people who could give. Why us? What should I do? And then an idea came to mind.

I decided to pray, "Lord, you know I'm married. Marilyn and I are one, so this is a 50/50 decision." My reasoning was that Marilyn was not going to want to part with the money we'd saved for furniture. New furniture was a big deal to her. I would tell her the story about the $5,000, and she would say no and we would be done with it.

Son of a gun, she shocked me. "Richard, if the Lord's suggesting that, we need to do it."

We said goodbye to our savings and wrote a cheque for $5,000 that morning and gave it to this stranger's missionary work. Go big, Richard. Who knew that three years later we would have three times that amount of money. I really wasn't accounting for what God would do. But I know our decision was right and we never regretted it. I learned that turning everything over to God, even savings for a good thing, is the best way to live. You can't outgive God. He is the owner, and we are the stewards. And in the decades to come we would follow the pattern God set for us, giving away millions to charitable works.

We don't believe that if you do something good for God, like being generous, God will do something good for you. We didn't buy into the idea of give so you can get. That's not how the faith-life works. In fact, we saw more than once that sad things can follow generous choices for God.

The generous will prosper; those who refresh others will themselves be refreshed.
— Proverbs 11:25 (NIV)

We moved into our new house in October. Marilyn was more than halfway through her pregnancy. The business was growing. Everything was humming along. My decision to turn everything over to God was working out better than I could have imagined. That Christmas, however, Marilyn became violently ill. She started seriously throwing up. When her sickness continued, we rushed to the hospital. We prayed for her to be OK, but shortly after being admitted she started to have contractions. The worst happened. Our baby died. We were far from OK.

Marilyn had been so looking forward to this baby. She had chosen the room for our second child and the new room where Kelly would sleep. She was figuring this all out in her mind and then all of a sudden there's no baby. Marilyn understands the anguish women go through when they are having a baby and then they're not. Suddenly you have to reverse all your thinking. Every change you make, you get thrown back into a state of depression and sadness. She was devastated. We appreciated our family, friends and pastor trying to help us get through, yet Marilyn still felt alone. People didn't know what to say and sometimes they said the wrong thing. Grief takes time. It becomes a part of the fabric of your life. We still wonder about the child we lost. Here again, we turned our broken hearts over to God. We didn't understand why we had to suffer through this tragedy. It didn't make sense to us. But we trusted God.

Then, in the early fall of 1974, Marilyn became pregnant again.

Lisa was born in April 1975. We were so happy to have a little girl. The all-Canadian family. We had picked out two names for the baby: either Melissa or Lisa. But she was a Lisa. It was a name that we loved. And her second name is Lynn. That's because all the women on Marilyn's side of the family have Lynn in their name somewhere. Some are Evelyn or Marilyn, and some of them have Lynn as their middle name.

She was a baby that had her days and nights mixed up. That was a rough go for a while at the beginning, but she was a happy girl, smiling all the time, cuddly to hold. We thanked God for adding her to our family.

Business continued to be profitable and growing. I would graph the growth on an office wall. 1000% growth looked great. Percentages are interesting because when they're small numbers it can look big. The incredible increases continued year after year. We expanded across Canada and had a view to go international. We were booming. So was our family. We had a new house. Marilyn was happy and I was happy because the students were paying the mortgage.

When we first married, we planned on having four kids. But after Kelly and Lisa, we were good with settling into life with two. Almost four years passed before Marilyn started to talk about having a third child. I said that if we go for three how about going for four? Marilyn made it clear that she couldn't handle a fourth with my business travel increasing and her being left alone for longer periods of time. So, we decided on three and along came Laura.

Knowing that she was going to be the last child, Marilyn enjoyed every moment of being pregnant with her. She soaked in everything. This is the last time for this, and this is the last time for that.

Naming her was another big deal. Marilyn loved the name Sarah and it was important that her second name be Lee, but Sara Lee was a cake and we weren't going to call her that. We decided on Laura Lee Lynne.

Even today Laura says, "Mom, what were you thinking? Laura Lee Lynne Magnussen." And Marilyn repeats that she loved the names Laura and Lee and there had to be a Lynne. But who could have imagined that Laura would fall in love with a guy named Josh Leyes?

When Marilyn went to the hospital to deliver Laura there was a problem with the anesthetist. They kept paging him and he didn't show up. They told her, "You've got to do this naturally."

Marilyn said, "What?! You've got to be kidding. I can't do this on my own."

I was there massaging her back. "You got this, Marilyn." Oh, if looks could kill. I knew she was in panic mode thinking about the big contractions.

The nurse encouraged her. "Just watch my lips and when I breathe, you breathe. You just breathe with me." She had her face right there with Marilyn. And that's what got her through. She did the breathing. Laura was the first and last natural birth. And that was the end of the beginning.

Before Laura was born, we decided she was going to go wherever we went. We had worked around sleeping schedules and naps and feeding and every-thing with the first two. Laura was going to work into our family schedule. Being with people was all Laura knew and interesting enough, she is the most social of all three of our highly social kids.

Marilyn and I were partners in everything. Our faith, our family and we co-owned the business. Wisdom from the Old Testament says, "A cord of three strands is not quickly broken" (Ecclesiastes 4:12, NIV)

A cord of three strands is not quickly broken.
— Ecclesiastes 4:12 (NIV)

The symbolism of three strands can be used to represent a wife, a husband, and God. Three strands intertwined into a braid is not easily unraveled. That was good news when life unraveled around us. The growing pains of a family and a business would be sustained by our faith in God.

Chapter 3, Growing Pains

Being overwhelmed is a scary feeling. Life and business will challenge you with multiple, complex demands. One day you hit the proverbial wall. That breakdown moment can become a breakthrough experience. You discover that what got you there isn't sufficient to get you where you want to go.

The pain of trauma, disappointment, and loss can take you out of the game. The scars are invisible, but the effects are real and lasting. The only thing that will sustain you in pain is strength at your core. True strength comes from God.

- Where does your strength come from?
- Is your core strong enough to sustain you?
- What are you discovering about your capacity and what you truly value?

4

FAITH THAT WORKS

ONCE A YEAR, MARILYN AND I WOULD TAKE ONE WEEK IN THE winter and go to Mexico. Just the two of us. We were apart so much because of the business. It was very good for our marriage to carve out one week by ourselves.

On one of those holidays in the late 70s, we were enjoying the beach with another couple we had met at the resort. They were very friendly. Marilyn was sitting with the wife chatting away. The husband and I were in the water. We tried body surfing, where you wait for a wave and ride it on your stomach into shore. There were some pretty big waves that day.

The next thing I knew I was lying face down in the sand on the shore.

My neck ached.

I couldn't get up.

Marilyn says she happened to look over and noticed that I was lying awkwardly, half in and half out of the water, and the other fellow was bent over me trying to help me. His wife said, "I think something's gone wrong."

I had ridden a wave and it had taken me too close to shore. The wave drove me headfirst into the sand and now I was floundering around. It was a good thing our new friend was a take charge kind of guy. He, his wife, and Marilyn moved me further onto the shore and then hurried to the hotel front desk where he told the clerk he needed an ambulance. There is an emergency out on the beach. But there was no ambulance. So, they called a cab.

Meanwhile, I was trying to get up and was staggering. And I knew that it was quite serious. We did everything we shouldn't have done with a neck injury. If you know anything about swimming and accidents and neck injuries, you put a person on a board, tie them down, and you're very careful with any movement. I walked from the beach to the hotel and into a cab.

We were still in our bathing suits. Marilyn got in with me and they took us to what looked like a military clinic. The guy in charge looked me over and said, "Yeah, you've got a neck injury."

I have never been in such terrible pain. They said, "You need to go to this larger hospital. We'll take you by ambulance."

I told them, "I'm in a lot of pain. You've got to get me something."

They said, "Well, we can give you these needles and if your pain increases, your wife can give you a needle." They gave Marilyn two big needles. Well, she'd never given a needle before. You've got to be very careful when you give a needle. You can't get air in a vein. I said, "Marilyn, do not give me those needles under any circumstance. No matter how much pain I have."

I had to get up on the gurney because they said I was too heavy. I wasn't really heavy in those days, but you know I was tall. So I climbed onto the gurney and they got me into the ambulance. Once Marilyn was inside the ambulance, the driver sped off right over the curb with a bang. Marilyn was in shock, not knowing what to do. I just knew we weren't doing the right things. Nobody was taking it seriously or seemed to know what to do.

The area of Mexico we were in was hilly, so the gurney started rolling around in the back of the ambulance. Marilyn couldn't control it. And I had this vision. Do you remember The Three Stooges? I looked out the windows of the back door and imagined the gurney hurtling out the door and down the road like some crazy skit in a comedy movie. But Marilyn was increasingly upset because she couldn't control the gurney. I had one arm that was paralyzed. So I said, "Throw that arm out the little window on the side of the ambulance and my armpit will help secure the gurney for you." That's what she did and that helped to stabilize things a bit. It was just awful.

They took us to the hospital and that was disastrous. They took an X-ray and said, "We don't see anything wrong with his neck." Then they explained,

"We're just a sort of outpost hospital," which was an understatement. "You need to fly to Mexico City and see a specialist. You can get better X-rays there."

There we were in our wet bathing suits. Even though we were in Mexico, it was winter. Marilyn and the interpreter had to take a taxi back to the hotel to get some clothes. She really wasn't in a good state of mind gathering things. She grabbed clothes and toiletries, put them in bags, changed her clothes, and headed back to meet me. She had to dress me because I couldn't dress myself. That's when she realized the pair of jeans she had hurriedly grabbed for me were her jeans. She had to go back on the street with an interpreter looking for a pair of pants so I could get on a plane with more than a wet bathing suit.

If I could have, I would have laughed when she got back. She ended up with these flour sack-cloth-kind-of painter pants. I'm so tall and that was all she could find that were long enough. They didn't even have a zipper. There was a drawstring. Luckily, she had grabbed a sweater because it was kind of chilly that evening. Off we go to the airport in the ambulance. It only got better.

We arrived at the airport and the airline wouldn't let us get on the plane with my injury. My neck was flopping around, and I later learned my ligaments were torn. They needed a doctor to clear me. Over the PA system they asked if anyone was a doctor. A guy came in and said he was a doctor. I was relieved when he rolled up a towel and taped it to my neck. That was the first time someone knew what they were doing. That helped a bit with the pain. It gave me a bit of stability because I had to sit in the airplane seat. I couldn't lie down. Takeoff was rough and bumpy. They should never have moved me from the horizontal position with a neck injury.

We finally arrived in Mexico City and, once again, no ambulance. We got into a cab and asked to go to emergency at the hospital. That was a mistake. The cab driver took off like a race car driver and we had to keep saying, "Please slow down and take it easy. He has a neck injury." The driver spoke only Spanish. I don't know what he understood, but we did a lot of hand language. You know, sore neck, slow down. He would slow down for a while and then he'd race again. We did the very worst things you could do for a broken neck.

By now it's 10 at night and we're whizzing through these back streets of Mexico City. We're getting even more nervous about the whole scenario. We finally arrived at the specialist's office. I remember the moment like it was yesterday. There's a guy painting the door frames. It's 10 at night. He's unshaven. He was using a big brush you would use for wallpapering. And he was painting the trim. I thought, *You got to be kidding*. I wondered what the care was going to be like.

We get into the building and they put us in a room with a bed on a cobblestone floor. The toilet was overflowing. It was all green, running underneath the bed. Above us was a lightbulb that was pigtailed. That's about as safe as, well, it's not safe. An aide took us to the X-ray room and guess who shows up? The guy taking the X-rays was the same guy painting the door trim. I looked around and no one had a protective X-ray shield on them, including the doctor who had also been painting the wall. That wasn't good. The doctor said he couldn't see anything broken. "But you go to a hotel and I will get you a brace for your neck in the morning." We're in this strange place, not knowing anyone. And all we know is this doctor that we're relying on and he's trying to get the meds I need so that I could go back home.

We took a cab to the hotel and the next morning he brought a brace. Back in those days, braces had little clamps that secured the brace around the neck. On one side the clamp worked but the other side didn't. One side would stay up, the other side would fall down.

We decided not to call home to our family, not wanting to worry anyone. What could they do anyways? We wondered whether we should fly home right away, but we did have two or three days left on our holiday, so we decided to stay at the hotel and go back later. Can you imagine that? We were not as experienced travelers back then as we are today. We would do things very differently. I know from taking a Red Cross swimming course that I should have been stabilized.

The first night in the hotel I could feel every movement on the bed in my neck. The second night the whole bed started to tremble and I thought it must be an earthquake. It was just like someone was at the end of the bed shaking it. When we woke up the next morning, Marilyn asked how I slept. I said, not very well. We had an earthquake last night. And she said, "I didn't feel any earthquake." And I said turn on the TV and sure enough, they had recorded an earthquake overnight.

We had left our station wagon at the airport in Toronto. When we got back, I laid down in the back of the vehicle and Marilyn drove us home to Kitchener. When we arrived, she pulled into the garage and opened up the trunk for me to get out. Marilyn's mother was taking care of the kids while we were gone and said, "Oh my goodness, what is going on?" We hadn't given her any warning. Our poor mom. She would babysit so willingly and at least twice we returned home in a desperate situation.

Another time we were in a snowstorm and a hotel fire. We couldn't get from the airport to our home, so we had to stay in Toronto in a hotel because the highway was shut down due to snow. And when we did get home, Marilyn was still in her nightclothes because there had been a fire in the hotel, and we had to leave everything behind. We had a friend pick us up in Toronto and bring us home and Marilyn is still in her nightclothes. Mother asks, "What is going on now?" That's life with the Magnussens.

The morning after returning from Mexico, we drove to the Kitchener-Waterloo hospital. They took X-rays and put me in traction right away. The X-rays showed that I had cracked vertebrae six and seven, and I tore all the ligaments in my upper shoulders. The doctor told me I was half a millimeter from being paralyzed from the neck down. Half a millimeter!

The doctor was astounded when I told him what happened. He surmised that at the very last second I must have turned my head. That's what saved me from totally shearing my spinal cord. I learned that the spinal cord has a texture like toothpaste. It's not like it's a firm cord. They kept me in the hospital for a few days. Two of my friends visited me and they were trying to cheer me up. I don't know if they realized the severity of the problem, but they were trying to make me laugh, which was really not good. There was a little card with the patient's name on it on the hospital door. My buddies drew a little torpedo surfer on the card. While they were there, the specialist came in and he was not impressed. He gave us a lecture about not taking my injury seriously.

When I was released from the hospital, the specialist gave me a neck brace, and I was supposed to wear it for six months. Then he surprised me by adding, "You're going to have to wear this brace for the rest of your life when you're in a car because of any potential risk of whiplash."

That specialist didn't really have a personality at all. He was a little abrupt and grumpy and never explained anything. And I wasn't in the mood to ask questions. Within a few months they took more X-rays and he said, "You don't need to wear the brace anymore." And I thought, *That's strange.* But he wasn't the kind of guy you could drill into with questions. So, I followed the instruction and stopped wearing the brace.

Two years later, I happened to meet my GP on Chicopee Ski Hill in Kitchener-Waterloo. He introduced me to his wife. "This is the guy I told you broke his neck. He shouldn't be walking let alone skiing." So that was my first realization of how the doctor saw what God had done. I thought, *Gee, that's really something that he's introducing me to his wife by making that statement.* I'm sure it was impactful for him because he remembered the extent of my injury.

Twenty-five years later, a different GP, Dr. Bennett said, "I want to have another MRI of your neck and see what the status of it is."

I had no headaches. I had no side effects other than when I was wearing the brace. The brace tilted my head forward, which I'm confident gave me a forward neck protrusion. I used to rest my chin on the brace and it wasn't good to have that posture.

The MRI came back. Technicians are never supposed to react to anything they see, but this technician asked me, "Who fused your neck? It's the most perfect fusion I have ever seen, right and left side of six and seven."

And I told her, "It never was fused."

And she said, "You're kidding!"

I said, "What you're telling me is why I didn't have to wear a brace."

I explained to her that I was supposed to wear a brace anytime I was in a car. And she said, "Well, you have a perfect fusion left and right on your vertebrae. They are perfectly fused together."

The only conclusion is that it's a miracle. God certainly took care of me even though I didn't get it confirmed until 25 years later. If I had known that then I would have drilled into the doctor with questions. But I was relieved that everything was working again, including my arm that had been paralyzed. I never had therapy on my upper back. I should have gotten therapy. Since my neck is fused, it's a little harder for me to turn left and right than the average person, but the doctor many years ago told me to exercise in the shower first thing in the morning and I do. I was advised I could probably anticipate some arthritis in the neck. The exercises must keep it flexible. I do notice that my neck aches a bit at the onset of a cold or a flu, but that is all. No complaints here.

God did marvelous things for us that we didn't even know at the time. And later we realized what a beautiful job God did, even with the things that we weren't aware he was doing. That accident had all the potential of being disastrous. I could have been in a wheelchair for the rest of my life.

I got out of the hospital, wore the brace, and went back to work right away. In the early days after my accident, I wasn't able to do physical work like cutting plywood, but I was able to get more and more into the small things of office work. I have a clean bill of health, and for that, I'm eternally grateful.

The older I got the more my faith in God mattered. What began beside the wine-colored couch in my mother's living room as a child was maturing into a solid foundation for living. My personal choices, our marriage and family life, as well as business decisions were directed by the wisdom I found in the Bible.

Chapter 4, Faith That Works

Every now and then, something special happens—something that logic or reason would tell you is either impossible or the odds against it are overwhelming. Something such as broken vertebrae perfectly fusing together without surgery. Maybe you have experienced something special that you can't explain.

- How should we characterize or classify seemingly impossible events? Are they miracles? Coincidences? Could it be that a coincidence is a small miracle in which God chooses to remain anonymous?
- Where do you see God at work in your life?

5

ONE IS TOO SMALL A NUMBER

ONE IS TOO SMALL A NUMBER TO ACCOMPLISH ANYTHING great.

I've seen that any success worth having arises out of relationship, delegation of responsibility, truth, trust, integrity, and high-capacity leaders. If the first law of real estate is location, then the first law of business is character.

Most leadership coaching focuses on building personal skills and knowledge. In our case, drawing on professional relationships fueled growth and helped the business surpass limits.

For our team to succeed, I needed A-players who produced results but would do so with humility. This combination of humility and professionalism kept our team united and working towards a shared goal—the success of Magnussen Furniture.

In 1977 it was time to enlarge our footprint. We sold the little 13,000 square foot factory that my dad had on Waterloo Street and put an offer on a 50,000 square foot building in the neighboring town of New Hamburg. Purchasing that building meant our overhead would rocket. I spent many evenings in my accountant's kitchen listening to him assure me we could do this. Finance at this level was an all-new frontier.

The building was owned by Electrohome. It was a furniture factory, which is what attracted us. The list price was $425,000. The floors needed repairing, and an adjacent storage building had to be fire-proofed to qualify for a lower insurance rate. I offered the owners $125,000. Much to my surprise they quickly accepted it and threw in a machine that was worth $100,000. At the time, it was a buyer's market and the loss we took on the sale of our factory was more than made up for by the purchase of the larger building.

The new facility felt cavernous for our small workforce of eleven full-time employees. It was desolate and empty at first and cost more to operate. More than once we wondered if we had made the right decision.

My dad was still involved in the day-to-day operations. He was building a 130-Pallet finishing line with three spray booths. The operation worked like a charm, as did everything he put his hands to. The business started to accelerate. Orders poured in. It was never boring at Magnussen; however, the demands on me were overwhelming.

I grew up doing the work myself, because when I started there were two part-time people. I made the furniture, sprayed the furniture, loaded shipments on the trucks for the train cars. I did everything in the business. From a very young kid of ten years old, I swept floors. I was never above doing anything. One day on the shipping docks I saw a guy struggling with a box. I went over and lifted it for him and threw a couple more boxes on the truck. It was good exercise for me. I appreciated the people on the front line working hard every day because I knew what it was like. They would see me do things and they'd say, "Whoa, why does the boss do that?" But it was my statement that we all do whatever we have to do to get the job done and deliver great customer service.

Pleasing customers was ultimately important; however, we had one customer who was very abusive to our people. They tried everything to make the guy happy. Finally, the customer service manager came to me and said, "This guy is always abusing our people. He has them in tears."

So, I called the customer and said, "You know we appreciate your business, but we cannot seem to meet your requirements. Our customer service people are trying very hard to give you good service but they get sworn at so I don't think we're a good fit for you."

I think my call took him off guard. He was a bully and, in his world, if you intimidate people you're going to get better results. Difficult people are difficult because difficult works for them. Long story short, he became a very good customer and no longer abusive. The customer care people thought, *Whoa, the boss is willing to get rid of a customer to protect his people.* I only had to do that once in 47 years.

I've learned over the years that a lot of leaders want to hire less knowledgeable people so they don't lose control of their business, but in reality, that stifles whatever you're trying to do. We wanted to hire the best to be the best.

I was praying about how to go forward under the load I was feeling, and a man's name came to mind. Ed Lehman. Ed ran two Flexsteel upholstery plants. He also knew wood production. Ed was good. We met in his office, and I asked him to come and work with me. Long story short, he thought Magnussen was a small operation and so he declined.

I was crushed.

Ed had the same strengths as my dad and was much younger. He knew technical production, was a leader in manufacturing, and a creative thinker, and would have helped us incredibly. We really needed his kind of expertise.

About a year later, I was driving home in the evening, feeling discouraged. Not that business wasn't good. It was so good that I desperately needed somebody to keep up with the demand. I'd been talking to Marilyn about the situation and the pressure I was under. I needed someone that we could trust who knew the business and would be creative in manufacturing. For weeks I had been praying. I was praying again as I drove home. "God, I need somebody." I was almost in tears.

Who should I see on the side of the road trying to flag me down? Ed Lehman. Ed's hobby was beekeeping, and he had his bee hives along that road. I thought he wanted to show me his bees and stuff. I stopped and rolled down the window. He leaned in and asked if I was still looking for a person to hire. And I said, "I am." And he said, "I'm your man." And now I'm driving away from Ed with more tears in my eyes, only this time they were tears of joy.

Ed started working with us soon after that. He agreed to a salary plus bonus, as there was no way I could match his current salary. I was thrilled to delegate all the production to him. Was that a coincidence? The timing was very, very clear. God answered my prayer.

My dad had been running the production management. That was his strength and his weakness. He was a perfectionist. That was good for results, but he would be hard on people. He wouldn't tolerate any imperfections. Dad and Mom owned a double wide mobile home in Florida, and they would go there for five months every winter. That was usually a time of peace on the factory floor. The year Ed took over, he set a new tone, worked with the staff, got things streamlined, and built some custom machines to make production automated. Everything was humming.

Then we ran into a little bit of trouble.

When my dad came back from his winter holiday in Florida, he went out on the shop floor. He loved talking, especially with Ed because Ed was German and had learned the trade in Germany. Ed and Dad really liked each other. But one day Ed came to me and said, "Look, I really like your dad, but either he has to run the production floor, or I have to run it, because he's giving direction to people his way. And you know, mine is a little different."

I had to talk with my dad.

I prayed about it and explained, "Dad, this is how Ed's feeling. He really likes you. He loves the discussions you have. But you've got to decide whether you want to run the plant again or you want Ed to run the plant."

My dad said, "Oh, no. I don't want to run the plant."

He wasn't aware of the effect he was having. But that was my dad. He was all in. If he saw something amiss, he would be there to point it out. And so, his willingness to let go was another answer to prayer.

Dad had laid the foundation of quality control, innovation, trust, and continuous improvement. Edwards Deming was an American quality control expert, college professor, consultant, and is the most well-known name in management. In 1947, Deming was invited by General Douglas MacArthur to help Japan rebuild their economy. He was so successful that thirteen years later, with Japan's economy booming, the emperor awarded him the country's highest honor. My dad had never heard of Deming, but when I became aware of Deming's work, I realized Dad modelled many of Deming's principles. One was the idea that small, ongoing, positive changes could result in significant improvement.

It's rewarding to see how the small changes we made in the 80s resulted in success and are reflected in how our company describes itself over forty years later.

We think our point of differentiation is our unique combination of heritage and vision. For the last 90+ years, we've built a rich history of crafting quality furniture at unbeatable values while embodying our core values of trust, honesty and respect. These are the principles that guide us as we design, craft, and deliver some of the world's most beautiful home furnishings. Put simply, we're constantly challenging ourselves to create furniture with the aesthetics, innovations and thoughtful design features that make stylish living easy. (https://www.magnussen.com/About-Us)

Today, our team, under the leadership of president and CEO, Nathan Cressman, my son-in-law, Magnussen Home continues to raise the bar of excellence. With a focus on continuous improvement and delivering unprecedented values, we're making our vision of fashion-forward product design, industry-leading fulfillment, and authentic customer care a reality. And the result can be seen in homes around the world that have been trusting the Magnussen Home brand for more than three quarters of a century.

I'm convinced part of the reason we have such a strong workforce of talented people at Magnussen Home is because of our values. Business is all about people, and people are all about relationships, and people are drawn to honest values, and in particular, people are drawn to humility.

All went smoothly again until years later when we started to import furniture internationally. Ed wasn't thrilled that we were bringing in furniture from Taiwan. I helped educate him on what was going on in the world stage of making furniture.

"Ed, here is what's happening in the market. Overseas, they're making chairs for $9.95. Can you make one in this plant for $9.95?"

Ed replied, "Oh, that's really going to be tough to compete against."

And I said, "That's what's coming down the pipe."

I think Ed saw the writing on the wall.

Ed's kids had moved to Kelowna, BC, and his wife wanted to be with them, and he wanted to be with his wife. Our work relationship ended but on good terms, and when I was to be given a lifetime achievement award, I asked Ed if he would be my guest at the event. In my speech I gave him a lot of the credit for Magnussen's success.

February 1980, I hired Dave Bast to be the controller for our business. I needed someone with strong accounting skills. I'd known Dave since we were teens. We attended the same church, volunteered in the Christian Service Brigade boys' program, I knew his family, and appreciated his personality. He was a graduate of Wilfrid Laurier University's business program, and I felt he would be a good fit. Dave had the capacity to handle the import orders and payments. He became responsible for all the bank letters of credit and tracking of shipments. That year we made $1.29 million in profit.

Dave managed Accounting and the office staff. We employed a bookkeeper and a receptionist to process orders, and then added more staff to keep up, and added a second story to increase office space. We looked at bigger computer systems to become fully automated. Back then we needed an entire room for a computer system that today would fit into a laptop. I trusted Dave completely. I turned over full signing authority to him. There would be stacks of cheques, but he signed them all and kept me in the loop with regular reports.

The business faced the danger of being bottlenecked, because I had my fingers in too many pies, but by hiring Ed and Dave, the daily operations were able to be delegated so I could focus on building the business.

In the early 80s, I started to see small amounts of furniture coming into California from Taiwan. The value was great, and I realized the potential risk to our then Canada-only occasional table business. If this foreign furniture took hold in our Canadian market, we would be in trouble. My sales manager and I hopped on a plane to check out the source of manufacturing. It was a high-quality product from some very good factories.

In 1981 and '82 we began importing furniture from southeast Asia. The import business took off like crazy. Dave had the capacity to handle the new load. He became responsible for credit letters and for ordering and tracking the items. I sent him to California to set up warehouses for our imports.

I would always tell others that Dave and I worked together. I would never say I own the company. I'd say that about any employee because I really wanted to promote team and working together. As we got a little larger, titles were required because people wanted to figure out what the responsibility of a company representative was. In 1986, with our US market expanding, I gave Dave the title Vice President of Finance and Administration, because it gave him more credibility stateside.

The first line of furniture we imported from Korea was made by Hyundai. Yes, the car maker. At the time they were into furniture and ship building. Asia was way ahead of us with technology. I came back from one trip to Singapore and told Dave, "You wouldn't believe what I saw. They have a machine that you can plug into a regular phone line and send a picture over it. It's called a fax machine." So, we bought one. It cost about $3,200. Dave was ever willing to help in ways that went beyond business.

I love boating. I caught the passion from my dad in 1966. He purchased a 17' catamaran in 1966 and over the next twenty years we bonded as sailors on that boat. I learned about reading the weather, and in particularly the wind on the water. These skills would later set me up well for managing larger power boats.

My other passion is spotting opportunities. In the early 90s, a friend of mine, Steve Scherer, a GM dealer in Kitchener, suggested I visit the Presidential Boat Company in Taiwan when I was over on furniture business. I learned that I could get a custom-made boat at a wholesale price if I could import it to Canada. So, I made a deal with the owner. We used what we learned importing furniture and started importing boats. Dave got involved, and he and Steve became my partners. Presidential Yachts was born.

Our import business secured exclusive rights for Canada. The boats they manufactured at the time—35', 37', 43', and 55'—were shipped on large ocean-going boats to New Jersey. I imported and Steve marketed. Once the boats arrived in New Jersey, they were trucked to Ontario to dealers set up by Steve. It was a fun kind of business, and profits from boat sales lowered my own personal boating expenses. I named my first custom-made 55' *President's Choice*. The 55' was too large to truck, so a group of my friends and I had a blast sailing it up the Hudson River from New Jersey to Lake Ontario and on to Georgian Bay. Our family used that boat, and it also became the show boat to help market Presidential Yachts.

The first two years of operation were incredibly successful. We imported and sold 35 boats. However, when our hobby started becoming more work than fun, we sold the dealerships to our main customer on Lake Simcoe.

After I left the import business in 1997 and built our cottage, I focused on watercraft that would be good for the cottage. I purchased a couple of Sea-Doos for the family. Our kids and grandkids all got their boating licenses in Ontario. I also purchased a 36' muscle boat with a top speed of 83 mph. It was a lot of fun for the more adventurous boaters, easily catching air on big waves. Not for the faint of heart. In 2009, with more grandkids around, I bought a 28' Chris Craft, driven by twin 350 mercury engines with a top speed of 55 mph. We still have the Chris Craft. It's in mint condition. Even though it's getting near being an antique, people think it's just a couple of years old.

You'll see a pattern developing of twin engines on our watercraft. It's a safety issue on big water like Georgian Bay. If one engine goes down, you can still get home. In 2016, the first home we purchased in Naples, Florida backed onto a canal. I bought a 24' boat with twin engine outboards. When we moved houses, I upgraded to a 38' boat. In 2022 I bought a new 43' Formula boat with quad 450 racing engines that can reach a speed of 72 mph. That beauty can fly.

I'm fussy about my boats. They go into a boathouse every night, waxed and taken care of. Marilyn is not a boat lover; however, she loves entertaining onboard. It's her gift. That's why she loves the 43' Formula 2022. It's built for entertaining, perfect for sunset cruise dinners on the Gulf of Mexico.

In the furniture industry, Magnussen is known for integrity. People listen to what we say and what we do. We weren't perfect by a long shot, and I don't know that every sales rep would always do the right thing, but that was more about ignorance than integrity. When I was in the showroom and overheard a salesman say, "That's great oak," but it was cherry, I never credited that as being dishonest. I would go to the sales manager or vice president and say, "He's a great salesman, but you need to work with him to learn the product." Trained employees who knew the product were integral to success.

I think people see a disconnect between what happens on Sundays at church and what happens on Mondays at work. For me they are seamless. What I learned and experienced at church shaped how I led the business. Here's an example.

A team from Life Action in the States came to our church for a series of meetings with families. I had never heard of them and wasn't all that interested, but our pastor was enthused about them coming and we wanted to support him. There was a service every evening and Marilyn and I attended all of them. I soon found out that God always looks deeper than I do.

One evening's theme focused on the value of a clear conscience. Attendees were encouraged to think about anyone we'd ever wronged, hurt, offended, or cheated and go to the person and say, "I screwed up." Immediately, one specific issue popped into my mind. In the furniture industry it is common practice to copy, as nearly as possible, the successful designs of other companies. I had recently taken a picture of some products from two companies and replicated them for Magnussen. I didn't even blink an eye because it was what everybody did. Now, my eyes were opened to this practice as God saw it: dishonest. Even though it was considered acceptable in our industry, I could no longer excuse the practice of stealing competitors' designs.

So, I asked God to forgive me. The next steps were to call the men whose designs I had copied, ask their forgiveness, and commit to making financial restitution. To me, this was more than improved business ethics; it was vital to walking with God in obedience.

At the time I was thinking, *This is going to be the end of me.* I remember anxiously having to dial the number of a business in Ohio many, many times.

Most executives are busy, and you usually leave them a message. But the crazy thing was I was able to get through to the receptionist almost immediately, and she put me through to the CEO. I explained the situation and apologized for copying the designs. He said, "Forget about it. Everybody does it; it's no big deal." I asked what kind of restitution did I need to pay?

He was surprised, "Restitution? Nothing really. If you want to, just donate to your favorite charity whatever you think the amount should be."

I knew what a royalty amount would be in our business and made a donation.

The second call to a West Coast company went the same as the first. I reached the CEO and explained what I had done. I think I caught him off guard. Who does this? Our industry is terrible for stealing ideas and never 'fessing up. This CEO expressed forgiveness and appreciation. He also declined financial reimbursement. "I appreciate your call. Just donate to your favorite charity."

It was a life lesson about integrity. God, my partner, honored the choice to be honest. The bonus was that I learned that copying generates lower margins; new designs generate more profit. In the long run, honesty and integrity made us far more money. With better designs we had a better product, and we weren't forced to sell on margin. When you produce a knock-off you have to sell it cheaper than the creators. Having original designs means you can be the leader on the price because that's the way the system works.

Originality may be costly or take more time, but it is worth it in the long run.

People with integrity walk safely, but those who follow crooked paths will be exposed.
— Proverbs 10:9 (NLT)

The founder of Life Action used the story of my experience in his talks as an illustration of the value of a clear conscience. They published my story in one of their training manuals. I guess people would be challenged to consider their own behaviors. I often wonder how many people got a clear conscience because of that story?

About six years later, our CFO came to me and said that we had overlooked a $20,000 invoice from a supplier. I said, "Dave, you go back and check, triple check to make sure we didn't miss something." He came back and said, "The numbers are right. We missed paying." I said, "Then pay it and let them know it was a slip-up." That happens. But just because a slip-up goes unnoticed doesn't make it right, even if the supplier wasn't aware and wouldn't notice that small amount amongst millions of dollars. But Dave knew. More importantly, I knew. Inaction wouldn't stand at Magnussen.

When God began to deal with me about integrity, He got to the root of the matter. God's way works. Our company was better for it.

I learned to hold on to a relentless determination to do what is right, not what is easy.

The Life Action family event showed me there were changes to be made at home as well. I had been a good provider but was an absent husband and father. I was working far too many hours, and my family was suffering for it. I began to see that God could take care of our needs and our business. I didn't need to be at the office all the time. I cut back on work hours and invested that time at home.

Trusting God has a profound effect on interpersonal relationships. First and foremost, God wants our relationship with Him to be right. Before we ever try to give or do anything for God, His primary concern is for us to be right with Him. That requires surrender. Once we are right with God, other relationships become what they need to be.

A business with a good upside can attract a lot of attention. Palliser Furniture in Winnipeg was a hugely successful, family-owned furniture manufacturing business. They were our western competitors. Their story was a lot like ours. Abram DeFehr immigrated to Canada in 1944 and began making furniture pieces in his basement. Within a few years the business moved from the basement to a chicken barn, which became Palliser's first factory. The principals were Mennonites with a solid reputation. In the 1980s I took a call from their head office asking if there would be any interest in us selling Magnussen Furniture to them. Would you come out to Manitoba and let us pitch you an idea?

I had no interest in selling, but you can only act on the information you have, so Dave and I flew out and listened to the proposal. They loved the import side of our business and made a tempting offer to buy me out. The substance of the offer would have relieved the pressure on my shoulders, taken care of our little family and set me up for life.

Dave and I had talked about what might happen on the flight to Winnipeg. I might find working for someone else very challenging after having free rein as an owner. And how the vision for Magnussen to grow an international footprint was just taking shape. We were staring exponential opportunity in the face. He was right. Their offer paled in the long run compared to the wealth Magnussen built. I would have left a lot of money on the table.

Vision and leadership. Those were two words I often heard at award ceremonies. In 2010 the Canadian Home Furnishings Alliance honored me with a Lifetime Achievement Award. Laine Reynolds, the board chairman, cited "vision and leadership" in making the Magnussen Home Furnishings brand a significant resource in the industry.

Focusing on growth and expansion led Magnussen to become a global residential furniture company, Canada's largest supplier with distribution centers in California and Vietnam, approximately 300 team members, including the sales team and head office, managing 10,000 contracted workers globally, selling to 3,000 customers in more than 20 countries, and finding homes for 125,000 pieces of furniture a month by 2017.

What's most important for a leader is the ability to manage change. Change is the only thing that is consistent. Managing change has a lot to do with vision. When you know where you're going, adapting to change can propel you to increased success. Facts are your friends. A leader's first job is to know the facts and define reality. Employees aren't going to do that.

Very early in my career, I learned the principle of measuring the critical things so that we weren't working on emotion. We were working with facts. Reliable metrics enabled us to continuously improve quality. Because we were meticulous in our documentation, we knew where to look to solve a problem. When a customer service person noticed there were damaged corners, repeatedly, on a certain product on a certain SKU, we knew we had a packaging problem. They documented that and then every month that report would go overseas to the managers responsible for those SKUs. They made improvements to solve the packaging problem. We were known for having one of the best quality products in the marketplace. Returns in the industry averaged three percent. We ran around one to three quarters of a percent.

I get frustrated with people who can't make decisions. Big or small.

All through my career I made decisions based on what I knew and the counsel I took from others. But I could not be assured at the time that I was making the right decision. You make decisions, but it's not until later if you see the result you hoped for. Do the best you can with the information you have to work with and make the decision.

I looked to hire the best candidates available for a role and I was good at hiring but I didn't bat a thousand. If I had a fault, it was waiting too long before dealing with a poor hire. I gave people the benefit of the doubt. I don't have a problem with confrontation, but when it came to letting employees go, I would err on waiting too long. I moved one VP into the CEO role. That was a lack of judgement on my part because he wasn't CEO caliber. In hindsight I probably delayed too long moving him on to another opportunity.

And if a business decision could negatively affect the lives of our staff, my default position would be to delay.

During one three-year period, I ran the manufacturing plant at a loss of about $1,000,000 a year. Imports were more than making up for the loss but that didn't excuse my delay in addressing the issue. I had a hard time shutting the plant down. I tried everything to make it work. What I learned through the experience was the reality that when I had to lay them off, employees were three years older, and it became more difficult for some of the older ones to get new jobs. And because it was very difficult to compete, I was just fooling myself that we could turn the plant around. I intuitively knew that. I should have been more firm with myself and made a quicker decision.

You can learn positive lessons from choices you regret.

One is too small a number to excel. I learned the wisdom that including trusted advisors and an expert team in my life and business is what leads to success.

Chapter 5, One Is Too Small a Number

Acting with integrity means you value good morals and ethics and follow them in every aspect of your life. Integrity builds healthy working relationships because team members feel respected and know they can rely on you and on one another. How are you living out the ways of integrity?

- Are you honest with your friends, family, and colleagues?
- Do you keep sensitive information to yourself?
- Do you follow through on your promises to others?
- Do you give credit to those who help you, deserve recognition and contribute to maintaining a positive work environment?
- Do you lead by example and do the right thing no matter what?
- Do you stay respectful in moments of conflict or disagreement?
- Can you exercise patience and keep calm in challenging situations?
- Are you consistently kind without expecting recognition or a reward?

6

LIFE ACTION

MARILYN PUT HER SKILLS TO WORK ON THE BOOKS IN THE Magnussen office, but with each pregnancy she stepped back from the role. Once all the kids were in school, I said to Marilyn that we could really use her back in the office. She explained that she could come back but she did not like being the boss's wife in the office. Plus, if she did go back to work, I would have to take on some of the housework, do laundry, help with meals, and shopping. That's where the conversation ended. She is an astute communicator.

Marilyn loved being a homemaker. A lot of women couldn't understand that. "Seriously, what do you do at home?" She would tell them, "I have no problem keeping busy. I love being involved in my children's school activities." She would always be the mom that volunteered for school trips, or baking things, or having kids over. Home was her happy place. Still is.

When we hit fifty years married, we signed a contract for another fifty. Marilyn is my best friend.

People who know our kids ask us what our parenting secret was.

We're proud of our adult kids, but there was no secret. We were young parents, so we didn't really know what we were doing. We only did what we were raised with and what we learned at church and from the Bible. I don't really consider myself the best example of a parent.

My greatest contribution to parenting was marrying the mother of our children. Marilyn was a reader. She would have books stacked on her night table on the subject of parenting—ten best things you can do to raise your kids. Our kids have a good mom.

Charm can mislead and beauty soon fades. The woman to be admired and praised is the woman who lives in the fear-of-God. Give her everything she deserves! Adorn her life with praises!
— Proverbs 31:31 (MSG)

If there was a secret it was that we loved our kids enough to ensure that they understood the Bible and how it applied to their lives. Our children were given a foundation of biblical truths, principles, and values that shape their thinking and behavior to this day. That carried forward into the lives of our grandkids. We encouraged them to be people who loved and respected others, chose not to make judgements, and would be the first to forgive. Here's where it helps to remember that in the Christian life, success isn't defined by having it all together, or enjoying material wealth and blessings. Instead, it's about being in a relationship with Jesus who created us, and stewarding what He gives us. Not that God measures success based on our behaviors. There's a religious system that says, "Work hard to earn your rewards." God says, "Be rewarded by receiving Jesus in simple faith."

Marilyn and I were always in agreement when it came to the kids and if we weren't, we would discuss it together. In some families, a wife will have one way of raising children and a husband has another and it's very conflicting for the kids. Marilyn and I saw eye to eye on most things and even if we had different approaches, we backed each other up. I was the authoritarian and Marilyn was the listener. I was quick to lower the boom on the kids and send them to their room. Marilyn would go and sit in their room and say, "I want to hear what you're feeling, why you're angry." That partnership worked well for us.

Weeknight family mealtimes were a priority. We couldn't have dinner together every night because of my travel, but that was time together that we did our best to protect. We must have built enough good memories because our kids prioritized their own family mealtimes when their kids were growing up.

"Her children arise and call her blessed; her husband also, and he praises her: Many women do noble things, but you surpass them all."
— Proverbs 31:28-29 (NIV)

Skip was our wild child.

He was a free spirit, a German Shepherd; the one and only dog we owned. He came into our lives when the kids were old enough to promise they would take care of a pet but still young enough that care and training fell on me. He was an outside dog, content to stay in his kennel until I was around to let him out. He'd tear up the yard having fun with the kids, never paying any heed until I spoke to him. When I purchased our first boat, that spelled the beginning of the end for Skip. He didn't like water. Marilyn didn't want a dog on the boat. When a neighbor's Doberman Pincer figured out a way to free Skip from his kennel and they ran away together, it seemed we had a solution. Until the phone call from the Humane Society.

It seems like Skip's accomplice had gotten away with the crime, but Skip was behind bars. The kids and I drove over to bring Skip home. We waited in the lobby while a worker went to fetch our dog. A mom with five little kids poured through the door and into the lobby. The kids looked sad, and the mom looked frazzled. She explained to the receptionist that their German Shepherd had gotten away. Her kids were heartbroken. Had they found their dog? At the same time, Skip was brought into the lobby. The opportunity was right in front of me, so I went over to the woman and said, we're looking for a new home for our dog. His name is Skip. For $25 you could take him with you. The money wasn't the issue, I wanted to attach some dignity to the moment. Right then and there we sold our dog. The kids watched Skip and his new family get into their car and drive away. And that was the end of our dog days.

With my overseas travel I was away from home a lot, but Marilyn kept me well informed about how the kids were doing. When I was home, I made a point of showing up at their sports or other events. My kids and I went out for fun date nights. Those were opportune moments to steer conversations to the areas where they needed some help.

We formed our family around faith, church, and principles from the Bible that we modelled for our kids. Life Action conferences at our church were family-oriented with practical insights on parenting. I learned that being authoritarian was not the best way to raise children. Rather than say, "This is what you're going to do in our house," we were encouraged to explain biblical principles, and model them for our kids and let them decide how they would respond.

Our pastors taught our congregation practical ideas about healthy family life. They told us that when teens go through tough decisions, parents do them a favor by helping them become independent problem solvers. One of the initial ways we fostered independence was to offer our teens three choices of activities that we were comfortable with. No matter which one they chose, we were good with it. They were happy because they got to make their own choice. It was a win-win.

In high school, Kelly thought he wanted to join the police force as a career. He was in a co-op class, and the school arranged for him to work in a halfway house that was run by Ray of Hope, a Christian organization. The first thing he had to do was read the files of all the kids. And he came back to us and said, "You know what? Those kids don't have a chance, their home life is horrible."

Life with our kids was fun. People have an impression of me as a serious, buttoned up, suit-and-tie guy, but our kids knew I could be silly. I've been known to "dance" on rare occasions. We couldn't get enough of doing things together. Now we love life with our grandchildren when we can be together. One Christmas the whole family watched the movie *Dumb and Dumber*. I laughed so hard I was crying. Bring me a bucket of KFC or buy me a Taco Bell gift card for Christmas, and I'm all set.

The kids were all Magnussens, but they had different personalities.

Laura is more like me. We love our space. Large rooms with natural light. I taught Laura at a very young age the proper way to dock a boat. Most boaters would throw their lines on the dock, tie off their boat, and leave the lines in a mess. I showed her how to work with every single line, so they had nice little coils. That was her job.

Opportunities to lead organizations gravitated to Laura. She was asked to chair the board of a private school in Kitchener. They loved her work because she was a get-it-done person and administratively strong. She has a lot of wisdom for her age.

Lisa is more like Marilyn. They have so much fun throwing parties and entertaining. Both love Christmas and decorating to the nines. Lisa's the artist. The interior design of their home in Greensboro was featured in a city magazine. The editor walked through the home and photographed much of the décor and decorations for Christmas.

Kelly is his own man. From the moment he learned to walk, Kelly was a tease. One night he came home from his summer job working construction. He sauntered into the kitchen where Marilyn was making dinner. As he went past her, she noticed little gold, round earrings in each earlobe. She did a double take. "Kelly, what have you done?"

"Oh, yeah," he says. "I got my ears pierced on the way home from work today."

"What were you thinking? You know that boys don't pierce their ears in our family!"

He laughed.

Marilyn was infuriated. Kelly knew full well not to get his ears pierced. We had talked about this. He knew better.

She said, "Kelly, I can't believe that you would be so disobedient and then laugh about it. Wait till your dad sees what you've done."

I came home. We all sat down at the table for dinner. I prayed over the meal. Marilyn couldn't contain herself any longer.

"Richard, do you see what Kelly has done?"

Now all eyes were on Kelly. What did he do? Then I saw the earrings.

"Kelly, what did you do?"

He waited until my blood pressure started to rise. When I motioned to stand up, he pulled them off and laughed. It turned out that they were just copper wire that his co-workers had shaped into earrings. His boss was a good friend of ours, and he thought this would be a great scheme to get a rise out of me. It worked. Fooled me. They sure looked like real earrings. Kelly thinks he's a trickster. He loves to tease.

I have been known to be stubborn and insensitive at times. Marilyn wanted me to take her to a production in Toronto called *Joseph's Technicolor Coat*. She purchased tickets. I wasn't impressed. "Would you please not buy tickets for me for these things? I don't like them. I don't want to go to them. Just take someone else if you want to go." I was in a cranky mood. Marilyn was a little ticked at me. But off we went to Toronto.

The show was surprisingly entertaining. It was about family complexities, and I could see some of our family's issues. There were some funny moments that took the seriousness off some of our family stuff that was worrying me. At intermission I told Marilyn, "The show was amazing! I love it. Let's get the CD." She smiled at my change of heart.

Another time Marilyn wanted to see a live presentation on our way home from the annual furniture market and visiting the kids in North Carolina. The presentation was in Pennsylvania. Here's one thing about me. I like to get to a destination as quickly as possible. No stops. We don't get off track. Marilyn says the event is only a little bit out the way. Five hours is not a little bit. But Marilyn really wanted to see the production, so, off we went. I quite possibly muttered under my breath a few times on the drive.

The production was about the life of Joseph from the Bible; different from the one in Toronto but equally entertaining. It presented Joseph as the annoying second youngest brother of twelve. He irritated his siblings to the degree that they wanted him dead. They threw him into a pit and sold him to slave traders. He ends up in an Egyptian ruler's household, is falsely accused, and sentenced to prison and, in an unexpected turn of events, is appointed second in command of Egypt by the Pharaoh. He saves his nation and forgives his brothers.

Not that our circumstances were anywhere close to Joseph's, but we could empathize with the complexities of his family situation. The story was an injection of hope for our future. It reminded us that God can take all the stuff that you think is going horribly wrong, and he works it out for good. For Marilyn and me it was an eye-opening experience that reminded us that God is going to look after us and make everything beautiful in his time.

In the Magnussen family, the time for kids to get their driver's license was on their sixteenth birthday and not a day later. There was no discussion about it. They took driver's education in high school. Shortly after each one got their license, they became the designated drivers to take me to the Toronto International Airport for trips to Asia. My departure times were usually late at night, so they missed rush hour traffic, but Toronto wasn't Kitchener and high speeds and transport truck traffic dissuaded people we knew from venturing into Toronto. But not our kids.

Kelly broke ground for his siblings. I loaned him the family car to train in and use after he got his license. My parents were like that. My dad let me drive his new Plymouth Satellite, which was a good-looking car. I think he had only owned it for a couple days when I asked if I could use it for a date. He said, "Sure," because that's the way I was treated with everything. I appreciated the confidence that my parents had in me, and I gave them no reason to be concerned. And neither did our children. Marilyn and I were in absolute agreement that the kids would grow up with our trust and opportunity to develop responsibility. When our kids showed an interest in spreading their wings, I was glad to be their wingman.

Kelly was fourteen when he took an interest in dirt biking. We both got dirt bikes so that I could ride with him. Dirt bikes were great for developing driving skills because they were off road. Beginners learned to judge distance and how to safely adjust to sand or rough terrain. Kelly was athletic and skilled up very quickly. We went out one Saturday with a bunch of dads and sons, and I was leading on the first ride. After that, Kelly led every time. He was quick and confident.

I had bought a Jeep for the kids. Kelly took it on a date and ran into a problem. He got into an accident, took the bumper off our vehicle, and damaged another driver's car. Fortunately, no one was hurt except for Kelly's bank account. The repairs cost him $1,700. I remember the amount because that was what he had saved up from his summer job. That hurt Kelly, but not as much as us. He paid for his repairs and the other guy's repairs. The kids understood that we paid for the car and insurance, but they had to cover gas and driving violations. Kelly wiped out his complete earnings paying for the damages. I still feel how hard it was for me to see him having worked faithfully all summer and then losing all the money. I could easily have paid the bill, but Marilyn and I talked about it and our conclusion was that in letting him go through the pain we might save his life from a next time if he realized accidents are costly.

The kids loved the novelty of the Jeep, and even I used it sometimes. In the long run it proved to be bad on gas but good at economic lessons. The kids had to pay for the gas, and it was a gas guzzler, so they said, "Dad, we need something more economical." It was costing them a fortune. We traded the Jeep for a Mazda. Less fun but more money at the end of the month.

People sometimes wondered if I was using good judgment with giving the kids so much responsibility at such a young age, but in chatting as adults, they felt good that we trusted them with the family car, among other responsibilities.

Try as we might, sometimes our unintended example was what not to do or how to behave. But that's OK. Life Action reminded us that no one is perfect, everyone is better with help from God and their friends.

Chapter 6, Life Action

Can a happy family life co-exist with a successful business career? We didn't set out to answer that question. Looking back, the answer to us is clear—it can.

- How are you prioritizing your life?
- If you have a family, do you prioritize mealtimes? The family that eats together is healthier and happier. Family mealtimes do several things:
- Build relationships. Eating together helps build a close relationship with your children. It gives everyone in the family a chance to learn more about each other. Turn off the TV and don't answer the phone during mealtime. Instead, use this time to talk, connect, and make memories together. It's a lesson your children will use for life.

  - Promote stability. Eating with your child helps them think things are OK. It sends a message of family stability.
  - Practice social skills. Eating together as a family gives your kids a chance to learn and practice their social skills, table manners and conversation skills.
  - Check out the Purdue Extension Nutrition Education Program: https://eatgathergo.org/gather/benefits-of-family-mealtime/

Note: link addresses may have changed after publication of this book.

7

UNDER CONTROL

I'VE NEVER SEEN MY FAMILY SO TERRIFIED.

They sat stunned, shaking in the kitchen, as I made my way out of the house to an elders meeting at the church.

Our kids hadn't seen or felt rage. For that matter, Marilyn had never felt that level of intensity from me. I mistakenly believed that it would take a long time for my fuse to get lit. Not that night. Was my behavior an echo of hearing my dad from so many years ago, sitting at the top of our second story stairwell?

My upper body strength is good, but even I was shocked by how easily the countertop of the kitchen island came loose in my hands.

We were standing in the kitchen, me at one end of the kitchen island and Marilyn at the other. The kids were sitting down. The countertop didn't come off totally in my hands, but it would need some serious repairs. So would our family.

I was dealing with a lot of pressure in the business. And now I was late for the elders meeting. Marilyn was on me about something. No excuses. Pressure goes with the role, and I usually handle it well, but not that night.

I lashed out at Marilyn, I am ashamed to say. I've never done it since.

On the walk to the car, I cooled down and thought, *What in the world are you doing, Richard?* The ironic part was I'm getting in the car to go to a church meeting to serve as an esteemed spiritual leader, a model of maturity and Christian character. I was trying to further God's kingdom, I had just disrespected my wife, and my kids had witnessed it. You can't stuff that kind of experience back in the box.

I certainly wasn't proud of my behavior, especially because one of my favorite Proverbs is, *"Sensible people control their temper"* (Proverbs 19:11, NLT).

I apologized to Marilyn that night, and she forgave me, but the wound went deep.

The next day I apologized to the kids.

I hope that incident is a forgotten moment deep in the oceans of our kids' memories, surfacing only as a reminder not to beat yourself up for being imperfect.

There are no perfect parents or spouses and certainly no perfect Christians. There's a joke that says if you're looking for the perfect church and you find it, don't join or you'll ruin it.

Wisdom sees trials as opportunities. Challenges and even setbacks are parts of growth.

> *Whoever restrains his words has knowledge, and he who has a cool spirit is a man of understanding.*
> *— Proverbs 17:27 (ESV)*

It's easy to lash out at somebody who's lashing out at you. I've had to bite my tongue more times than I can count. But I keep reminding myself, *I want to be above this.* I'd like to think that as you grow older, you're not quite as quick to say something that's sharp and cutting.

We had a manager who worked in Creekside Church's office. In the early years, Creekside Church leased a building and sub-leased extra space to other businesses. I was the elder entrusted with overseeing the facility and supporting our employee. The landlord was renting some office space, and he was giving our manager some grief, so I told her to set up a meeting with him and I would find out what his issue was.

The landlord came in a little charged up and defensive. He started attacking me verbally, making outlandish accusations. He levelled a lot of stuff at me. I'd never met the guy before. So, I let him go on for a while and then I said to him, "I apologize. I sure didn't want to give you that impression of our church." That took the wind out of his sails and we ended up having a good meeting. He agreed he would do some things and we got where we wanted to be.

We came out of the meeting and our manager said, "You apologized, and you did nothing wrong."

And I said, "Well, I was apologizing for anything that might have given him the wrong impression of our church." I said I was willing to take that to get this guy back on track.

She said to me, "I could never do that."

And I said, "Well, I don't have a problem taking the risk of listening."

She was more interested in the truth, that the guy was a jerk, and I didn't need to apologize.

A fool is quick-tempered, but a wise person stays calm when insulted.
— Proverbs 12:16 (NLT)

I learned in customer service training that when a customer is flipping out, you let them talk. That way you have a better chance to bring the upset customer down so you can deal with the issue. Had I gone head-to-head with him, I guarantee you we would not have gotten the result we wanted.

There is nothing that can be done with anger that cannot be done better without it.

There is good customer service advice in the Bible.

If it is possible, as far as it depends on you, live at peace with everyone.
— Romans 12:18 (NIV)

It's no fun to apologize when you've done nothing wrong. But as the leader, sometimes you have to take one for the team.

Not long after we bought a penthouse condo in a newly developed tower, the builder went bankrupt, and the building went into receivership with a bank. There wasn't even enough time to form a condo board, it was all so new. The bank assigned a trustee who was unbelievable. The builder had shorted us. We tried to negotiate to get the furnishings, the hallways, and the lobby done, but the trustee wanted nothing to do with us. He was serving the bank's bottom line. They wanted to get their investment out. I understood that.

We had an issue with one of the corridors. When people opened the door to the corridor the wind would grab the door and knock people over, and ripped it off its hinges. Some of the owners reported it to the trustee with no response. People were getting very angry. They said, "We're going to call the newspaper and tell them what a bad place this is." I'm thinking, *If you want to destroy your real estate value, just go and do that.*

I took it on myself to call the trustee. I explained how the broken door was a danger, residents had been injured, and owners were getting frustrated because there was no action. He said, "Well, why are you calling me? Who are you?"

"I'm one of the condo owners."

"You know, you don't have any authority."

I said, "No, but I am concerned about people getting injured with that door."

And he said, "Don't worry about it. We have liability insurance."

I said, "I assumed you would have liability insurance to cover it. But I'm worried about the people that are getting injured." I explained what happened recently to a grandmother, her daughter, and grandson. He started swearing at me. Intimidation was apparently his choice of style.

I learned in customer service to just let the customer vent for a while. Difficult people are difficult because difficult works for them. On he went until finally he played his trump card by threatening to take me to court for interfering.

When he seemed to be out of words, I said, "You know what? That's a good idea. I'd like to stand in front of a judge, and you explain your position and I explain mine."

I called meetings to set up a condo board. There were five of us elected and I ended up the president. Marilyn said, "You love this stuff. But all these people had invested their money, and they were being taken advantage of. Including us."

Then the trustee tried clawing back parking spaces that we had purchased with our condos because too many parking spots had been sold. The penthouse came with two spots which gave it higher resale value. He tried to claw one of ours back. There were eighteen of us in this situation.

So, I called a meeting.

"Look, I don't think this is right; we've paid for these parking spots, we own them, and they want to grab them. I think we need to get a lawyer involved to make our representation."

Their response was interesting. "Lawyers are expensive. We can't afford one." That separated out those who were serious about taking on the bank appointed trustee. Of the original eighteen, only five of us wanted to take it to the next level. It was going to cost about $10,000 each for a lawyer. There was a lot of wisdom among these guys. They were all businesspeople. The five of us went to court for a hearing.

The judge was so upset with the trustee, he tore a strip off him. "These people have more invested than the bank does." He railed on the trustee. I almost felt sorry for him. I couldn't keep the smile off my face. The judge ruled against the trustee and awarded them all the costs, so we didn't have to pay the legal fees. We won the case and the five of us got our parking stalls back. I had fun.

We got what we wanted. The bank had to pay us a lot of money to redo all the halls, the carpets, the lobby, so I felt good about that project. And units in that building have gone up in value.

It upset me that the trustee was taking advantage of people. Certainly, I was an owner, but I saw how those people were floundering about how to get it fixed. Calmness and taking the bully down with just words that were measured but very direct, that brought him to a stop. We never had a problem with him after that.

A gentle answer deflects anger, but harsh words make tempers flare
— Proverbs 15:1 (NLT)

I took a chapter out of a story in the Bible about a leader named Nehemiah. He rallied people to rebuild the walls of Jerusalem while they were defending themselves against their enemies. They worked with a trowel in one hand and a sword in the other and rebuilt the wall in fifty-two days. He had to stop often to encourage them and keep the people on the same page. People naturally lose their vision when there's sustained pressure.

When the dust settled, Marilyn and I bought the penthouse in an adjacent condo tower. Our former tower had 148 units and this one had 204 units. Our neighbors asked why we were moving. I said I just liked another challenge.

Not too long after moving in, I was elected to the board and asked to be president. I wouldn't say I deliberately do these things; I just want to protect my own investment. I do deal with a lot of leadership issues, so I'm not getting rusty in my later years.

Keeping my emotions in check and being under control built a reputation for me of solid, stable thinking and leadership. Self-control is a discipline worth working out.

Chapter 7, Under Control

Other than talent and opportunity, what makes some people more successful than others is self-control—the capacity to regulate attention, emotion, and behavior in the presence of temptation. "You only have control over three things in your life—the thoughts you think, the images you visualize, and the actions you take" (Jack Canfield, *The Success Principles: How to Get from Where You Are to Where You Want to Be*). Practising good habits is more impactful than having strong willpower.

- What habits are serving you best in regulating attention, emotion, and behavior?
- What habits in this chapter could you find useful?

8

OUTSMARTING PROBLEMS

THE APPLE DOESN'T FALL FAR FROM THE TREE. NOT THAT WE had apple trees on our acreage, but we did have trees and they had a lot of leaves.

I am meticulous about yard care. Some might call it obsessive.

My friend Byron Paulus worked with Life Action. When he came to our church on behalf of Life Action, I invited him to stay in our home for a few days. We were living on Riverbank Drive at the time. The first thing Byron noticed when he parked in front of the house was how the lines in our lawn were unbelievably straight. He loved the attention to detail and told the story to his office staff when he got home.

Every time I went to the States for a Life Action board meeting, his staff would joke with him, "Richard's coming? Those lines will be straight for him, we promise you."

In 1981, when we bought our larger plant in New Hamburg, we decided to move homes too. The kind of property we were looking for was not available in Waterloo, so we settled on an acreage near Cambridge, Ontario and built a 5,000 square foot English Tudor house. We lived there for 19 years. Laura was two; Lisa was six; Kelly was nine.

We landscaped gardens in and around the walkways to the front door, around the side of the house, and the back of the house. As a gift to us, my dad had installed a large flagstone patio that was quite extensive. We planted gardens all around it. There was no shortage of weeding, mowing, and raking as the kids got older.

I always look at how I can outsmart a problem.

The kids used to fight about who did what with the yard work. So, I color-coded the two acres of our property to stop the fighting. I have been known to be very orderly. I may be a slob with my clothes, but not with my lawn. I drew out a little sketch of the house and all the gardens and randomly plotted all the trees. Then I took three different shades of highlighter and color coded the landscaping assignments. Kelly would be one color, Lisa would be another color, and Laura would be a third color. The gardens and lawns in an associated color would be the ones each child would be responsible for. Worked like a charm. When Kelly became a dad, he told me that he copied that idea with his own kids because he was tired of hearing them fight over chores.

I would check the weeding every week. All I had to do was look at the colors and I'd know which child to talk to if their weeding wasn't done appropriately. But that left little arguing between them over whose responsibility it was.

Our kids will tell you they have many memories about lawn maintenance. Good memories.

They all had weeding, but Kelly, being the eldest, got to use the ride-on mower. Lisa used the push mower. Laura was the youngest, so she didn't get any of what she thought of as fun roles, like riding the lawn mower. Raking and weeding went to her.

One weekend, Lisa wanted to go to Canada's Wonderland with all her friends, but she had put off cutting the grass and by Saturday morning it still wasn't finished. Her friends waited while Lisa cut the grass. It was wet. A mower clogs when the grass is wet and long. All her friends were standing around, impatiently waiting, but she finished her work and off they went. I asked her when she was in her late 20s, "Was that over the top?" And she said, "No. I was a procrastinator, and I got that message clear. I had all week to do it."

I thought maybe I went over the top. I could have done the lawn because I like yard work. It's a no brainer type of work. But me doing it wasn't helpful to her. And that's the part that's really hard, because it's easier for me to do it than have my kids do it. There is a cost to go through the pain of helping kids understand the discipline of keeping commitments.

When I was a teen, it wasn't an option to not cut and weed the grass. I remember being at the cottage. There were a bunch of weeds in the lawn. My job was to keep that lawn weed free. That weekend at the cottage there were lots of friends including some of Marilyn's family and everybody was going to the beach. It was hot. But I hadn't finished my weeding. And I'm talking about a lawn that wasn't big, but it was full of weeds. I had to dig them out with a little trowel. And so that's what I was doing when my mother said to my dad, "You've got to give Richard a break." But no break came. And, like Lisa, I have no hard feelings. There is more to disciplining children than corporal punishment.

Discipline your children, and they will give you peace of mind and will make your heart glad."
— Proverbs 27:17 (NLT)

Laura can't shake the memory of one year when she had the responsibility of raking the entire backyard, which was almost half the property. Not quite an acre, but it was a good portion. She was a teenager. She didn't really feel like doing it and put it off until the last day. I would give the kids deadlines for when I would want the lawn work completed. Usually, the deadlines were the end of the week, but if there was a bigger project, like raking, then I would give them a date. And by that date they had to have the task finished. I wouldn't nag them about getting the work done. Even if they saved it for the last minute, that was fine. But it needed to be done on time.

Laura procrastinated until the last day. She went out to do her raking assuming it was not going to take very much time. The kids knew I would be inspecting their efforts. I'm particular about how a lawn should look. There is a proper way to rake a lawn. Good enough was not good enough. All, not most, of the dead grass needs to be raked up. Laura was not getting all the dead grass, so I came alongside her. She reminds me I told her, "That is not raking up all the dead grass. You've got to use more energy and power." I showed her how. If I remember right, it took her eight hours to finish the backyard.

One fall Saturday, the kids had finished their yard work. The lawn was meticulous; freshly cut, beautiful, green. No leaves. On Sunday we arrived home from church. The first thing I noticed was about ten leaves that had fallen from our tree in the center of the front yard. The kids remind me that I got out of the car and, rather than going into the house for lunch, I picked up every leaf. They thought it was so funny. What's the point? But to me, I like to look out and see a beautiful lawn and the lawn looked meticulous again. Now I could eat in peace.

As the kids got older, Kelly got a job, Lisa graduated to the riding lawn mower and Laura got to use the push mower. She had to go around every tree and get all the areas where the riding lawn mower couldn't access. That was an intensive project, and I was very serious about it.

Guess what? The kids have grown up with homes of their own and they all like to keep a nice lawn. They have somebody that mows their lawns, but the grandkids do all the weeding. Laura and Kelly are just like me when it comes to managing their kids' work responsibilities around the house. They have their own gardens, and the kids are responsible for weeding every Saturday. And Laura and Kelly check their work. There's nothing their neighbors don't like about the way they take care of landscaping.

Laura was 16 when her siblings got married and moved out. Yard work became a bit much for her to manage on her own. So, I hired a lawn care business to do the lawn. That got her off the hook.

I saw everything we did with our kids as an education. We were preparing them for life.

Kelly, Lisa, and Laura were still little when Marilyn found herself on the short end of appreciation. I knew how hard she worked to make everything good for us, but she felt our older two weren't thankful for all that she did around the house. Not that Marilyn didn't love being a homemaker, and she wasn't complaining, but she was probably overworked, underpaid, and under-appreciated. When Mom's not happy, no one's happy.

I woke up one morning with an idea.

"Marilyn, you go to Florida and visit my parents. You've got to take Laura because I can't manage a baby but leave Kelly and Lisa with me."

The kids didn't seem to have a problem with it and Marilyn was ready for a break. Off she went to Florida with Laura. The kids thought it was going to be a piece of cake with Mom gone and Dad in charge.

So, I had a little meeting with them:

"Lisa and Kelly, listen. I'm working so I need your help to get things done. This is the deal."

"I want you to clean your rooms."

"We need to go grocery shopping."

"I'll rely on you to make the meals."

"We'll have to get the laundry done."

"I've got a list of other things for you to do that Mom always does."

They were old enough to be able to do those tasks. I wasn't trying to be like the military, but there was an edge to what I wanted them to feel.

Marilyn was good about having them make their beds and she taught them responsibility, but they didn't appreciate all she did as their mom. Kids will be kids.

By the end of the two weeks, when Marilyn came back, she got the biggest hugs and welcome home she'd ever felt.

Marilyn was happy.

The kids survived.

They understood and appreciated a little bit better what she did for them.

Mission accomplished.

There's always more than one way to outsmart your problems. The positive outcome is worth the effort.

Chapter 8, Outsmarting Problems

You can't make problems disappear, but you can train yourself to a point that problems don't get the best of you. Find the opportunity in a problem and you are more likely to find a solution. It's true that the problem isn't always the problem, it's how you see the problem.

- What problems are you facing?
- How could a change of perspective lead to outsmarting the problem?

9

THE WAY OF WISDOM

I WASN'T LOOKING TO MAKE A STATEMENT, AND SURELY wasn't out to build something monumental with Magnussen Furniture. I wanted to earn a good living for my family and had no aversion to capitalizing on opportunities.

Do you know people who limit their goals because they're afraid of making big decisions and, ultimately, are afraid of failure? Fail forward. That's my life philosophy. Only those willing to do so will survive.

To achieve big things, you need a sustained drive and single-mindedness focused on your work. Dave, a former employee, calls it "focused tenacity." God doesn't guarantee riches and success just because you work hard. But God gives you what's best for you. And sometimes that's tough times disguised as success. Miracles happen during our darkest times. We don't realize how big the miracles are until we look back.

Revenues at Magnussen Furniture Inc. and Presidential Furniture USA Inc., the Canadian and American sales arms, grew twentyfold between 1981 and 2001.

The Canada-U.S. Free Trade Agreement was signed by Prime Minister Brian Mulroney and President Ronald Reagan on January 2, 1988. The agreement ended the 15% tariff that used to protect Canadian furniture makers. With the breakdown of traditional protectionist trade laws, I knew we had to adjust our business model. We either had to compete or get out of business. Some competitors fought to preserve protectionism, but, having already travelled to Asia, I could see the future of furniture manufacturing was borderless. I refused to play ostrich.

As president of the Ontario Furniture Manufacturers Association, I pleaded for the industry to begin looking outside our own borders. Now only those moving to do so would survive. Those screaming "Put up the tariffs! Get out of free trade!" were going to get swept away by the flood. Canadian manufacturers were well protected by tariffs, so it was very easy to be complacent. I took a lot of heat in the meetings because I was the only one importing and manufacturing. They were ignorant about what was going on in the world of manufacturing because all they knew was Canada. Some went to the US to visit the furniture shows, but they had no idea what was coming internationally.

I chose to use the imminent change to our advantage and expand to the U.S. We launched a major assault on the U.S. market that I believed would see total sales double in three years. The move was especially bold coming at a time when plenty of Canadian furniture manufacturers had shut down because of high interest rates, tariff reductions under free trade, a stronger Canadian dollar, and other factors. We operated under the name Presidential Furniture and designed a new company logo with U.S. and Canadian flags merged. It was controversial, but it made us stand out. The amazing part is we got more business in Canada as well. We were making a statement that we could compete.

My initial foray south of the border was a money-loser. Magnussen expanded into the U.S. market to increase our volume and make us more attractive to manufacturers. However, when we made that decision, I chose not to use *factors* in the beginning, and I lost my shirt. A factor is similar to an insurance company. They act as middlemen who provide credit financing to retail suppliers.

Factors work like this. If I sell through a factor, I pay them a small percent. Then they approve the order to that customer because they know their credit is good. If they stop giving a retailer credit, it negatively influences the retailer's bottom line. They really control the credibility of retailers.

But when I went into the U.S. market, I didn't have a clue about that part of the business. A retailer might look good in the front of the store, but they may not be paying their bills. We don't use factors in Canada, so I thought we were good enough not to need them in the U.S.

Six months in we knew we had a problem. We were quickly awash in bad debt when some dealers took advantage of our ignorance. We shipped orders and we weren't getting paid. The terms were 30 days and it's not uncommon in our industry to pay at 60, but when it gets to 90 and 120 days, you know there's an issue. Our first step was to leverage the salesman and have him go back to the retailer. We tightened that up by saying, "If you sell something to somebody and we lose our money, you lose your commission." No one was happy until we started to play by the rules of the game and used factors.

The U.S. strategy paid off in the long run. The U.S. market accounts for 75 per cent of Magnussen Home's sales, 20 per cent comes from Canada, and 5 per cent of sales are international. After marketing studies showed that the family name and history had a great deal of respect on the global market, we rebranded to become Magnussen Home.

By 2016 Magnussen was in the top twenty wholesale suppliers in North America. The big guys were gone. I was leasing a 60,000 square foot showroom from Thomasville Furniture, the icon of icons in the industry. They had a great reputation. They were bought out by another big division, and they all went bankrupt. They had put $1,000,000 into a showroom that I got for a negotiated price. I woke up one day thinking, *Oh my goodness, you talk about change. Those guys were the giants, and we're sitting here controlling their location and featured at the furniture market in High Point, NC, which is the Mecca of the furniture industry.*

In the 90s we had a difficult time competing with pricing on Canadian-made products, losing $1 million a year on manufacturing. The losses went on for three years. At the same time, the Ministry of Environment said the dust collector in our manufacturing plant was creating too much noise. A residential neighborhood had sprung up around us. The neighbors were complaining. But the cost to relocate our factory would run into multi-millions of dollars. We had no choice. We shut down manufacturing and went 100% international, buying our occasional tables overseas, and eventually turning our factory into a rental commercial property.

I prayed a lot during that time, asking God why this was happening. But I later realized that God was closing doors of domestic manufacturing, and opening doors into the international world of business that I would have never imagined would be part of our small family business. We were able to offer new lines of residential furniture that today include master bedroom, youth furniture, home office, dining room, entertainment centers, and more. In 2023 Magnussen Home shipped 125,000 pieces of furniture every month, with sales to over 20 countries.

In 2006 I backed away from daily operations to focus more on non-profit dealings. Magnussen had a president and a CFO who worked very well together. That was good on many fronts. But the company took on debt, much larger than we should have. For many years we ran with no debt because we were small, but as we grew, we had to buy inventory and use credit. But I let that get away from us.

The effects of success can subtly creep up on you and before you know it, there's a liability. In Jim Collins' book, *How the Mighty Fall,* his underlying premise is that when corporations become successful or CEOs are successful, the success can lead to entitlement. It becomes easy to lose track of the factors that made them successful. Arrogance can take over. They believe in their own press and slowly begin to see the momentum of success erode and turn into decline.

North America was going into recession. It was a dark, difficult, and traumatic time. Our bank became concerned about world markets. They went from being happy to loan us millions to giving us just a few months to find another bank. But who wants to loan money to a leveraged furniture company when the world financial situation is so bleak? Business dropped 40% in just 3 months. We were bleeding money. I wasn't sure if the business was going to survive. People don't have an appetite for furniture when the economy is tanking and they're thinking survival. Our lawyers felt we could make a case against the bank's sudden turn, but I was more interested in getting the business turned around.

We carried $35 million in debt. The only option I could find was to borrow money from a specialty company that dealt in high-risk companies at a cost of 18%. That wasn't much fun. Our company was suddenly in jeopardy. The bank was moving in on us and they wanted me to put in some personal money. My advisors, accountants, and lawyer said don't do it. They'll just grab the money and you'll still be in the same position.

I met with our management team and decided to increase my day-to-day engagement. The salespeople wanted me to get more involved as well. At that time my son and son-in-law were working for the company in the High Point

North Carolina office. We had some challenging meetings. Our VP of operations was Russ Langford. Russ was a major part of improving our business in the area of supply chain management and just-in-time delivery. Russ and I sat and put a plan together to lower our costs. We had to lay off some sales management. The president decided to move to another company. Decreased staff meant the rest were shouldering extra responsibility. Sales continued to struggle because retailers could not increase furniture inventory like they did in the good times.

At the same time, we were setting up a 650,00 square foot distribution center in Vietnam. That allowed us to offer 24-hour service for customer care. We lowered our costs and our inventory and figured out a profitable way to ship small orders, combining them with other orders in a 40-foot container.

Our operations manager came out of a chemical business which supplied chemicals just-in-time. He said we could do the same in furniture. We took a risk on the system and guaranteed five-day delivery to customers in Toronto. Our large warehouse in California was transformed into the hub of delivery operations. The overseas containers would be delivered to the hub. From the containers they would be loaded on trucks for delivery. We used two drivers per truck so they could drive all day and all night. We managed to ship small orders for many customers by consolidating on the containers from our large inventory. The timing was perfect. In 2007, our industry was not supplying just-in-time so that gave us a big edge. We had good quality furniture AND we could expedite delivery.

Most of our competitors thought I was going to go bankrupt over storing fifteen-hundred 40' containers' worth of inventory in the distribution center in Vietnam. The humidity is so high that there is a significant risk of growing mold on furniture. But we engineered the space with 75 enormous dehumidifiers running 24/7 which pulled 500 gallons or 1,893 liters of water out of the air a day. An idea to sell the water as distilled water didn't pan out. The good news was we didn't have mold growing on our furniture like some manufacturers did because of it sitting too long in storage.

Kelly and my son-in-law Nathan had major responsibilities by this time, working out of the Greensboro marketing office. They would call me every week and ask, "Are we going to make it?" I said, "Well, I think you might be having to settle back in Canada and work out of this office." I knew they didn't want that, so I would add, "Just pray about it. If we don't make it, God's got another plan. Let's work hard, let's focus, and let's get costs under control."

Then a remarkable thing happened.

We had been in a thirteen-year long lawsuit with a supplier in Toronto who had not fulfilled their contract with us. A number of times I told our lawyer just to drop it, but he assured me we would win. Suddenly, out of the blue, our legal case was settled, the very week the bank gave us a deadline for the money. The settlement we received was the exact amount the bank demanded we pay. What a relief. A coincidence? I don't think so. Everyone in management knew the timing of this was not a coincidence. There is no doubt in my mind that God had orchestrated a miracle. He used the tough times to teach us a lesson about pride and the need for us to humble ourselves and let Him be the leader. God has been the one blessing us.

We paid off the 18% loan and got back to normal banking within a year. The bank saw we could supply just-in-time to our retailers. We gained a lot of business because we had set that up. We were growing quickly again.

It was a major turnaround in profitability. We got our egos out of the way, and things got back on track to the point where we could have easily let our egos take over again. It was such a stunning turnaround. The auditors wanted me to travel and speak about turnaround and give us an award. I said, "No thanks. We're going to focus on solving problems and keeping the business lean." I know it was God helping us. It's easy to say now that it was the best thing that ever happened, but that was the scariest time in our business. God was good.

A respected friend suggested, "Richard, you should try reading one chapter of Proverbs in the Bible each morning. There are thirty-one chapters in the book of Proverbs. Read the chapter which corresponds to the calendar date. Proverbs chapter one on the first of the month and so on. Then do that every month."

I started reading a chapter each day. What I discovered was an incredible source of wisdom. The principles in Proverbs are timeless, good for ancient leaders and modern entrepreneurs. I was reading words that made sense; practical wisdom about relationships, integrity, dealing with conflict, principles of life, marriage, parenting, success, and business.

Getting wisdom is the wisest thing you can do! and whatever else you do, develop good judgment.
— Proverbs 4:7 (NIV)

Many people I interact with feel the Bible is not relevant. However, when I ask if they've read it, the answer is no. It is consistently the #1 best-selling, least read book. It's surprising how popular leadership experts teach content that echoes what is in the book of Proverbs.

Aside from the Bible I wasn't a big book learner, but back in the 80s I purchased a copy of Tom Peters' bestseller, *In Search of Excellence.* I was impressed with what I read. His lectures were popular with CEOs and when I heard Peters was coming to Toronto to speak at a business event, I decided to go. The tickets were $1,600 each. I thought, *That's a lot of money to spend,* especially in those days. But I wanted to hear what he had to say.

Peters moved across the stage like an evangelist. He was enthused about people taking ownership of their job, giving employees responsibility, and being clear, upfront, and trustworthy with them. But what I realized was that his principles of excellence were all in the book of Proverbs. I wondered if Tom pulled his content from the Bible. The teaching that was appealing to these CEOs was supported throughout Proverbs. The book is full of state-of-the-art management tips. I was sending some of our staff to leadership conferences and after a while I discovered that all they were getting was Proverbs, just in different formats. Here I was spending all this money, and I could have just given them the book of Proverbs to read.

Our staff were willing to die on a hill for me. I wanted to make sure it was the right hill.

Magnussen prided ourselves on an open management environment. We insisted that everybody at the table was free to share their view of things. Intel comes from the front lines way better than what is issued from an ivory tower. Getting out, talking to the employees, as well as taking time at every monthly meeting over pizza was dedicated to getting feedback. We did an employee survey every year and although the responses reminded us that we weren't perfect they gave us an understanding of what people were thinking. We published the results as a matter of transparency and followed through on as many suggestions as were viable.

We started a monthly newsletter and monthly meetings because of employee suggestions. Those made us better. The thirty-five to forty team members in our Canadian office heard me talk about the business issues and the CFO would talk about how things were going financially.

We cared about people. When I'm asked about the Magnussen cultural values, my response is simple: I loved our people. That may sound naïve, but our team felt it. They knew that I had people's interests at heart. We made the effort to put people in a position to do things that they loved to do. Our bottom line was people. That came through in more than our profit-sharing system. Employees aren't motivated by money. *The Harvard Business Review,* as well as all the data collected by multiple agencies through the century will tell you that. Employees deserve a fair and generous wage or salary, but dollars aren't the reason people will take the next hill. It wasn't all roses, as some of our employees were creative about how they could make money by not working. But for the most part, people helped define the hill and we took it together.

I believe a good life is a result of good habits. Much of what we do every day is habitual, we just aren't aware of the habits. I wanted my kids as well as my employees to have a good life, so helping them practice good habits was important to me. I can be a force when I get an idea in my head, and I had an idea for my kids. I told Marilyn that I was going to get the kids up early on school mornings so we could read Proverbs together before breakfast. Marilyn isn't a morning person, but she joined us each day.

Kelly, Lisa, and Laura Lee were less than enthused that first morning. I told them the night before we were all getting up fifteen minutes early starting tomorrow morning. Why? "To read Proverbs together. It will be good for you." They tried to tell me that it was so early, sleep was important for growing kids, and they would be happy to read anytime later in the day.

The next morning, their alarms and my fatherly help roused them out of their beds fifteen minutes earlier than usual and we all went downstairs with some grumbling to the living room, plopped onto the couch and I read chapter one from Proverbs.

> *"The proverbs of Solomon son of David, king of Israel: 2 for gaining wisdom and instruction; for understanding words of insight; for receiving instruction in prudent behavior, doing what is right and just and fair; for giving prudence to those who are simple, knowledge and discretion to the young—let the wise listen and add to their learning, and let the discerning get guidance—for understanding proverbs and parables, the sayings and riddles of the wise.*
>
> *The fear of the Lord is the beginning of knowledge, but fools despise wisdom and instruction."*

See, you don't want to be a fool.

After a few mornings of this new routine the kids knew I was serious. They knew that from previous experience that it was best to humor Dad because he wasn't going to be deterred. And after a while they seemed to take to the habit. Not that there wasn't occasional complaining or yawns that punctuated the reading. They were up with their alarms, went downstairs with their Bibles to the living room, and dug into their verses.

We read one chapter of Proverbs each morning. If the calendar date was the 17th, we would read Proverbs chapter 17. Some mornings the kids were assigned their turn to read out loud. Sometimes they read the chapter to themselves. Every morning, they chose a verse from what they read and talked about what it meant to them. They would share why they thought it was important or what they could gain from it or what they could work on in their behavior. Then we would get on our knees and pray. After that was breakfast and then rushing off to catch the school bus. We did that every day that they were in elementary school and through high school.

As a parent it's hard to tell when you're pushing your kids too hard. You don't want to turn them off something that is good. Decades later Laura pleasantly surprised me by remarking that she had fond memories of those times. She liked that I led by example and never wavered even if they sometimes whined.

I read a chapter of Proverbs almost every morning for a solid ten years. I don't have the 31 chapters memorized but I know the principles. And when something comes up, I can go to several proverbs and apply their wisdom to my circumstance. They are the foundation of understanding life. When I give a birthday card to my grandkids I often write in, "Proverbs chapters 1 & 2," reminding them about the importance of gaining wisdom.

Life and business advance at the speed of trust.

In the early years of Magnussen Furniture, I had no idea what that would mean for our bottom line and the test of trust that God was about to put me through. But the way of wisdom got me through it.

Listen to the words of the wise; apply your heart to my instructions. For it is good to keep these sayings in your heart and always ready on your lips."
— Proverbs 22:17-18 (NLT)

Excellence is about valuing people. When you invest in your team's development and well-being, you'll find that they contribute to increased productivity and, in turn, organizational excellence. Excellent organizations maintain a strong corporate culture centered around core values. They don't rely solely on bureaucratic processes but encourage employees to embody these values in their daily work. The same works in your family.

- How are you intentionally building trust in your organization?
- How are you building up the people in your life?
- Have you ever read the book of Proverbs in the Bible? Consider reading a chapter a day, as my friend challenged me to do, and as I led my children in doing.

10

COUNTERINTUITIVE LEADERSHIP

EARLY IN MY CAREER, I WAS TOO CONCERNED WITH HOW I appeared to others.

When the business was doing very well and we were making millions, I drove a car that I thought made me look humble. It was a Bonneville, a sporty car, one of GM's better models. I could have driven a nicer car, but I wanted to show that I was humble. One day it hit me that my motives weren't right. Driving a less expensive car to look humble was anything but humble. That wasn't honoring God. It was naive.

As I look back on my life, I believe God has been teaching me, and moving me towards greater and greater humility.

Humility gets a bad rap. People often have the impression that humility means to diminish yourself or think less of yourself, so it's not a quality they respect. Humility is perceived as meekness and weakness. But I'm proud to be associated with the word humility.

Humility is not low self-esteem or self-loathing. It's not thinking less of yourself, rather it's thinking of yourself less. Humility recognizes our inherent worth and seeks to use whatever power we have at our disposal on behalf of others.

One way of defining a word is to describe its opposite. The opposite of humility is pride, self-centeredness, and a me-first attitude. Humility, on the other hand, is gentle, teachable, and servant-hearted. Next to love, it is the most common virtue mentioned in the Bible.

I would argue that many of us are drawn toward humility even as we are prone to pride's grip on our lives. We find humility attractive. I am not there yet, but the older I get, the more I have come to realize the power and strength true humility can bring to life.

It's very hard, if not impossible, to sustain corporate excellence without humility. Ego gets in the way. EGO stands for Edging God Out. Jesus is my model of a humble attitude.

> *You must have the same attitude that Christ Jesus had. Though he was God, He did not think of equality with God as something to cling to. Instead, he gave up his divine privileges; He took the humble position of a slave and was born as a human being. When he appeared in human form, he humbled himself in obedience to God and died a criminal's death on a cross. Therefore, God elevated him to the place of highest honor and gave him the name above all other names, that at the name of Jesus every knee should bow, in heaven and on earth and under the earth, and every tongue declare that Jesus Christ is Lord, to the glory of God the Father. (Philippians 2:6-11, NLT)*

The benefits of humility are endless.

Humility enables us to be content with things we cannot change like certain physical abilities, appearance, or IQ.

Humility enables us to accept people without unhealthy judgement.

Humility reduces the pride that sparks the hurt we too easily feel when we are not appreciated or recognized.

Humility gets us off the hamster's wheel of chasing more and more stuff, and more and more recognition, so that we can feel valued.

Humility keeps us from the drive to impress.

Humility means acknowledging that I don't have all the answers and that there is always a new perspective to learn from.

Humble people lack arrogance and the need to defend what they might feel ashamed of. They can own up to their mistakes and ask for forgiveness when they mess up.

There is a verse in the Bible that explains how God works: *"He guides the humble in what is right and teaches them his way"* (Psalm 25:9, NIV).

I can't spell worth a hill of beans. I'm a terrible speller. My friends tease me about that all the time. I just say, "You know I can't spell." Living humbly is easier than spelling humility.

Golf is another of God's ways to keep me humble. My son-in-law, Josh, shows golfers how to improve their game. My grandson Hayden is an up-and-comer. Kelly is a good golfer. I've tried golfing. I suck.

The last time I golfed was with Kelly, Josh and Nathan at a course named Kiawah following a High Point Furniture Market show. Kiawah is not an easy course. It's on an island and features the most seaside holes in the Northern Hemisphere. I can hammer a ball a long way; it just doesn't go where I want it to go half the time. I usually lose a lot of golf balls when I play Kiawah, but the last time was probably my best round ever. My boys got me a caddie, who really improved my score. They then made a remembrance of the game by getting me the 18th green flag and presented it with their signatures and a score card. I had shot a 44 on the front 9 holes. The flag is hanging in my garage. I said, "I can't do any better than this. I'm done."

I'm happy to cheer on Hayden as he pursues his love of golf. If you make it far enough in high school, you go to quarter finals, then regionals, and then the state final, which is the highest level. When Hayden was a 9th grader, he made it to the state final. Marilyn and I and Kelly and Kim were proud to follow him around the course. Recently, he won the North Carolina state championship for his age category and was named most valuable player for his school. It's fine by me that his grandfather can't come close to his expertise.

I've observed humility in the best of Magnussen's team members: everyday people who got the job done without drawing attention to themselves. My dad was like that. He was good at asking questions. I learned that behavior from him. There were many times in my journey when there was a situation where I didn't have all the answers. Admitting this and seeking others' input requires humility. My dad would say. "Richard, if you don't know something, you can get somebody that knows it."

My dad's words reminded me that I needed to hire people who are smarter than me. And when I say smarter, I'm saying more knowledge in a certain area. That is very important because you're only as good as the team around you. You can't be successful if you don't create a team environment or you're unable to mobilize people. However, humility could be considered counterintuitive when it comes to leadership.

At Magnussen we empowered our team by ensuring that their voices mattered. We were careful to reward them fairly. Any team member could come to my office and talk about anything. I didn't have an assistant who brought me coffee. I didn't want people to think I'm the big guy and everyone else must run around and serve me. Servant leadership is at the top of humility. That's a Jesus thing. He washed his disciples' feet. Now you can't get any more servant-oriented than that.

However, I didn't always listen to the whole story. Sometimes I'd respond before a person finished speaking. It was a bad habit, but it came out of working with people over a long period of time. I knew exactly what they were thinking and knew where they were going in the conversation. I quickly saved a conversation from taking two minutes that could take one. That was not smart on my part. Sometimes I give myself a biff on the back of the head for speaking too soon.

I'm not afraid to tackle anything, especially when it's in my wheelhouse. I'm confident in what I know, and I am very passionate about it. I genuinely love people, and I think I'm easy to get along with. So, I was caught off guard when the love of my life said one day, "Richard, you intimidate people."

"What?"

"You don't realize that there's a lot of people who hold you in high regard and put you on a pedestal."

I don't mean to be that way at all. I suppose being 6'4" and a bit overweight can have something to do with that.

I've learned that if you're not listening, you're not communicating well. In fact, half of effective communication involves listening. Successful leaders are usually great listeners who ask thoughtful questions because they are genuinely curious about others. I'm certain that people on our leadership team knew that I respected them, cared about them, and prayed for them.

I wanted to pull out the best in others.

I had a good rapport with my leaders. If they did want to take the conversation in another direction, they'd call me out. "Wait a minute, you're not listening to me." Type A people like me try to get to an outcome as fast as we can. But that can be a fault. At times I would love to steamroll over a conversation because I think some of the points being made aren't sound. But I try to listen, especially if there is a junior person at the table. They may not be heard, and we can miss the good they can contribute. When we are in larger meetings, in our company or in church, I look for the quiet ones and try to draw them out.

Good to Great: Why Some Companies Make the Leap...and Others Don't by Jim Collins, was the book that impacted my leadership thinking the most. Collins surveyed successful companies to see the kind of leaders who took them to the top. He discovered that it's not those with a charismatic CEO. Charisma is not an essential quality to build a prosperous organization. I liked that observation.

The concept of Level 5 leadership is based on empirical evidence. Over a five-year period, Collins conducted a research project to discover what distinguished so-called "good" companies from "great" ones. Collins identified characteristics of CEOs that are essential for the success of a company. Level 5 leaders:

- motivate the enterprise with "inspired standards" more than an "inspiring personality."
- have an almost stoic determination to do whatever needs to be done to make the company great.
- are lifelong learners, and passionately so.
- have a relentless determination to do what is right.
- go after results with a laser-like focus on the purpose of the organization.

Level 5 leaders know that adversity is a far better teacher than prosperity. Collins wrote, "The good-to-great leaders never wanted to become larger-than-life heroes. They never aspired to be put on a pedestal or become unreachable icons. They were seemingly ordinary people quietly producing extraordinary results." It is very important to grasp that Level 5 leadership is not just about ferocious resolve, an almost stoic determination to do whatever needs to be done to make the company great. It is equally about humility and modesty.

When Laura started her career in massage therapy, she had a boss who was bad at good judgment. Laura was so frustrated she would come home and want to talk with me about her day. I told her, "You got a great thing going here."

And she said, "What are you talking about?"

"You're getting a crash course here. You're learning all the things you shouldn't do as a leader. When you have your own business someday, you can apply those lessons."

That gave her a completely different attitude towards her circumstances. I think that's turning a negative into a positive. Always look for the good, which can sometimes be counterintuitive. I think that's good judgment. See the glass half full. How can we turn this negative into something positive?

That thinking served us well in building Creekside Church. Waterlines for fire prevention hadn't been installed in the area. The municipality insisted that Creekside put in water tanks at our expense for fire protection and they wanted them right in front of the building. Everybody was so upset. "They can't make us do that. It's a waste of money." So I said, "Well, wait a minute. What if we, instead of installing ugly water tanks, create an attractive little pond?"

The municipality was good with the idea and so we did it. What started as a problem is a positive for the church. We installed a small waterline that fed the pond to keep the water at full level, and it was less costly than the underground water tanks. When people drive in on the ring road, they see the building after their attention has gone to a pond with well-maintained gardens and landscaping. It's beautiful. There's even a waterfall and a warning sign posted in the middle of the pond: Danger Deep Water. We get so many compliments. Yes, it took a little bit of effort and a lot of volunteers and even more money, but we made the grounds look gorgeous. The area looks so good and most people have no idea of the original problem or the positive thinking that led to this beautiful outcome.

A humble attitude helped us turn the negative into a positive. Counterintuitive leadership follows the way of humility.

Humility is not thinking less of yourself, it is thinking about yourself less. Your focus is on others. Humble people live in accordance with their values and accepts who they are, with their weaknesses, strengths, and imperfections. They recognize when external resources are needed to achieve a goal. They know they don't know everything. They can identify their mistakes, take responsibility for their actions, and accept the consequences without blaming others. Finally, they have a sympathetic ear for different beliefs and differences of opinion and sincerely wish others well.

- Do you have the characteristics of a humble person?
- Which attributes do you feel you need to work on?

11

EXCELLENCE IS A REFLECTION OF GOD

FIRST BAPTIST CHURCH WENT THROUGH A SIGNIFICANT struggle at one point. The lead pastor had suddenly resigned and all of us deacons found ourselves on the frontline. My friend, Ken Taylor was the associate pastor and served with the deacons. When the going gets tough, I'm OK with it. I enjoy being a calming force during those kinds of times. Things felt a bit tense so I frequently tried to lighten the mood and remind everyone at the beginning of our deacon meetings that this could be our last time here. I don't think we handled things perfectly, which is pretty much normal for all of us, but I think we handled them well enough.

We were supposed to launch a church plant in 1987 but decided to delay because of the church's situation. We felt that it was not healthy for the church until a new pastor was in position.

First Baptist Church started growing again by 1989. It was time to move forward with the church plant. Creekside Church services were launched in February 1989 in the cafeteria at University Heights Secondary School with just over 130 people. Ken Taylor came with us from First Baptist to be our pastor. Our mission was to follow Jesus, love God, and love people.

We came out of a church that was hierarchical in terms of its structure and Pastor Ken was not wired that way. He wanted to create an elder team culture that was something very different from what I knew in church and in business.

It was hard to wrap my head around his model. Ken wanted to build a team concept where each elder had an equal voice, including the lead pastor. Decisions would only be made in unity. To me it sounded like an unworkable process. These were high expectations for a group of volunteer leaders, to sit around a table and agreeing on everything. I was used to making quick decisions on difficult issues as the leader.

I had my doubts.

"Ken, I don't think we can run a church this way."

At First Baptist we used the King James Version Bible, had Sunday School before church, and services where a suit and tie was the standard. I was forty years old. That was the only church I'd known since my nursery days. Ken wanted to change the culture of Creekside to be less formal, and more inviting for people who didn't go to church. He wanted to introduce small groups. We never had small groups. That was for other churches.

Grant Russell served on the board. He was a department head at the University of Waterloo and a consultant in the business world. I respected Grant for his expertise. He supported Ken's team concept and his ideas around church culture. I liked Ken's emphasis on relational unity. These were big shifts for me and Marilyn and our family, but I was willing to give them a try.

The elders didn't need to be unanimous about a decision, but we needed to agree to move forward on the decision. We had rare times when one of our elders said they didn't feel good about the decision and we said, "OK, we're not going to move ahead." We weren't focused on what would work or copying other churches. We wanted to do the right thing. "What is it that God would want us to do here?"

We respected each other, to the degree that we could take criticism from each other. That's healthy. More than once, Ken said to me, "I think you're off base here." We didn't always see eye to eye on issues, but we heard each other out. It made all of us better. I enjoyed serving in that role.

If you listen to constructive criticism, you will be at home with the wise.
— Proverbs 15:31 (NLT)

Marilyn and I were on the church planting committee. We had some initial concerns about our kids not having a youth group like the one at First Baptist. But they saw us every Sunday morning unloading equipment from the little trailer and hauling it into the school. They pitched in and their little hands carried some of the lighter equipment. They saw us being God-centered and committed. Things worked out OK.

For the next twelve years, we gathered on Sundays in rented facilities that included University Heights Secondary School, Bluevale Collegiate, Waterloo Collegiate Institute, and the Waterloo YMCA facility. It felt like the congregation had to check the Saturday newspaper ad to find out where we were going to meet.

We continued to grow, which meant we needed to find a larger site. Our long-term strategy was to rent. We never imagined we would own a building as Creekside. The problem was rents were increasing, and we quickly ran out of places large enough to accommodate our rapidly expanding congregation.

One thing I love about Creekside's leadership is the ability to adapt. We had a strategy, but we were OK changing it to accomplish the vision. We tried ideas and if they didn't work, that's OK, we'd change. It wasn't a hill to die on. So, we began looking for property and settled on four and a half acres in the city that we purchased for $550,000.

But Creekside continued to grow so fast we soon realized the property was not going to meet our long-term needs. Before we put a shovel in the ground the search process started again. We found a significant property that was on the perimeter of the city. Immediately some of the congregation saw a problem. "No one will be able to get there. The bus service doesn't go that far. You need a car and many of our congregants don't have cars." We ran a program called Celebrate Recovery, which helped addicts find freedom. It was very successful. In fact, Creekside was so successful we became responsible for administering Celebrate Recovery across Canada. However, in the early days, the people we helped all came by bus. How would they get to the new property?

We decided to partner with another urban church that was willing to host Celebrate Recovery. They had a building that was on a bus route. Our volunteer team worked along with their volunteers to continue the program. Win-win.

So, we flipped our downtown property for thirty-three acres on the outskirts and went through the re-zoning process to build a church. Leading change is not easy, but I like the challenge. Twenty years later that $550,000 property was worth over $16 million. Even if we were simply investors, it was a great investment.

I oversaw building the first phase of the facility which was completed in 2002. Phase one was a gym that seated 700, which we quickly outgrew and needed to add a second, a third, and then a fourth service. The second phase in 2015 added a west wing that seats 350, bringing our capacity to 1050. At the time of writing this book, phase three of the master plan is still conceptual and will include an 1800 seat auditorium. That capacity would make it the largest church in the area. We have a dream to grow even larger and make use of multiple service times. Our incredible children's pastor, Carolyn Burge, and her team had the most fun envisioning the kid's area. Think McDonald's or Disney times five. We built a huge indoor playground with little houses on the sides that are entrances to program areas for the smaller kids. Families love it. There is a coffee bar area, and during the week parents bring their preschoolers to play in safety, have a coffee, and socialize with other parents. That was all free to the community.

Some people think a fun play area for kids and their parents in a church is misspent money. I'm hard pressed to see how building something that's drawing parents and kids to church is a waste of money. Also, we like to help other churches, and we'll give them everything we've got. When other churches ask how we do things, we're quick to bring them in and share our plans and resources with them. I like the story of the two seas in Israel: the Sea of Galilee and the Dead Sea. The Sea of Galilee thrives because water comes in and water flows out. The fresh water is a habitat for life. The Dead Sea has no outlet. It is stagnant. Nothing lives in the Dead Sea. We want to be a church that is a conduit for others. God's blessings are to be shared, not hoarded.

Our leadership team was eager to learn and open to ideas from other churches, like Saddleback in California and Willow Creek in Chicago. Pastor Ken took our leadership to visit those churches a couple times. My first impression of Willow Creek was the grounds. Everything was done with excellence. Weed-free, well-maintained lawns, gorgeous trees, edged walkways, beautiful flowers. Somebody cared. I appreciate the appearance of a well-landscaped property.

Excellence is a reflection of who God is.

At Saddleback Church, I learned a valuable lesson about sustainable programs. Rick Warren says if you have a dream in your heart, start a ministry program. There were about 120 ministries at the time out of Saddleback. But behind the scenes his leaders told us, "That's Rick's position. We love his heart, but the reality is there's so many people who would like to start a ministry. We want to ensure that a ministry is sustainable. We've got a whole grid of questions that need good answers before we launch the ministry." They got our attention. We had excited people wanting to start lots of ministries in the early days of Creekside. We introduced the value of ministry sustainability to Creekside's DNA and the process helped us prevent a lot of crash and burn outcomes. There are fewer ministries, but we do our best to make sure the ones that start have the best shot at being sustainable. If something is worth doing, it's worth doing well.

Our dream at Creekside was to see leaders inspired and equipped, so they could lead transformation in our community. Investing in leadership is one reason Creekside invested in hosting the Online Global Leadership Summit. The Summit is an annual event out of Willow Creek that features dynamic pastors like Andy Stanley and Craig Groeschel as well as industry-leading experts like Truett Cathy of Chick-fil-A. The ability to live stream the event was a cost-effective way that allowed smaller churches with tight budgets to be able to get world class training in their own backyard. Dozens of volunteers and I were happy to play host to hundreds of pastors, board members, and volunteers at Creekside for this annual three-day event.

Being involved in a community-minded church is exciting. And fun! The facility enabled us to host a variety of events for the community. Creekside puts on an annual Princess party for dads and daughters. The little girls wear their princess dresses and dads dress up in suits and tuxes. In the summer we offer week-long day camps for kids. There are youth events, gatherings for women, singles, English as a Second Language for immigrants new to Canada. Our facility gets a good workout fifty-two weeks of the year.

Hundreds and hundreds of volunteers give themselves not just to what happens on our main campus or our campuses in Kitchener and in Chatham but to what happens in the community around us. Our pastor was at a meeting several years ago where officials were talking about what was going on in cities. The mayor of Waterloo and the mayor of Kitchener were at that meeting. Both mayors independent of each other said, "We are so thankful for Creekside Church and what that church is doing in our community."

The city wanted us to carve out space for a road through our property to provide access to new housing developments to the west of us. We'll end up with about 7000 people close to our church. Creekside owns thirty-three acres which could be divided into lots and provide great value to the church. A developer said he could build housing on the lots at our cost. One of our elders, who is a real estate agent, proposed the idea of using the lots to build affordable housing, which is a huge need in our area. We had previous experience in community development when we built a tower of apartments for seniors beside First Baptist. The government funded the project, and we manage the facility.

Marilyn and I are always inviting people to church. We had coffee with a neighbor couple, and my friend made a comment that he had no need for God. After a few invitations, he and his wife attended on a Sunday. He was blown away by how many young people were there and by how much joy he observed in the people.

Creekside's contemporary music brings in a younger demographic. I've heard older, disgruntled people say that's just not our style of worship music. Marilyn and I enjoy upbeat music. There's some music that isn't our preference, but our position is we're willing to give that preference up to see all these young people and university students coming to Creekside.

Thirty-four years after we launched, Ken felt it was time to turn the pastoral role over to a younger leader and transitioned out of Creekside. By then we had grown to 2500 people on three campuses in Kitchener and Chatham. Ken says that leading God's church is like surfing. God sends a wave, and we ride it.

To that end, one day I said to Pete, Creekside's new pastor, "I've been serving as an elder for 35 years. We need some young elders. I'm willing to step down to get younger ones into leadership."

He says, "But, Richard, you're not an old thinker. You think young." I'll take that.

Ken used his amazing gift as a teacher to impact thousands of lives. His ability to clarify and simplify the Bible helped many people experience Jesus and become disciples. His humility built the leadership of the elders team. Every elder has an equal voice. We do not go forward with a decision unless we're all on the same page. Sometimes that takes longer, sometimes more prayer, but we do not move forward with a decision until we are totally united. I have learned that it really is an amazing thing that has created unity in the team.

As the years went by and I observed the success of Ken's approach, I began to shift the way I was leading at work to bring people into more conversations to achieve that kind of excellence.

Iron sharpens iron, so a friend sharpens a friend.
— Proverbs 27:17 (NLT)

It was thinking excellence that broadened the horizon of Creekside, and it broadened the horizon of Magnussen from North America to the world. And excellence is, after all, a reflection of God.

Chapter 11, Excellence is a Reflection of God

Volunteering on the board of a church or serving in a local non-profit or charitable organization outside of your career is good for your soul. Practices and lessons learned will not only make you a better person, they can also help build a better business model.

- What volunteer opportunities exist in your community?
- How have organizations benefitted from your skill, expertise, and generosity?

12

INTERNATIONAL DREAMS

WE HAD BUILT A TRADITIONAL FURNITURE MANUFACTURING business and were considering pivoting to international importing. I truly believed both the business and impact opportunity were immense but so was the risk. At that point, I had a multi-million-dollar company with employees and profile across Canada.

In 1983, Magnussen became the first company in Canada to venture into the international furniture market.

I hired a manager named David when we first went to Taiwan. He was my manager in Asia for thirty years. Right at the start I said to David, "You need to tell me when I'm wrong because I don't know the culture and you do. You won't help me by telling me what I want to hear. I've got to know when I'm messing up."

In Asia, an employee does not tell their boss what they think or offer suggestions. The boss is the boss. I was used to hiring smarter people than me who could think for themselves, and I depended on their expertise. Advising me was very hard for David, but over time he saw that I was serious and sincere and made the adjustments.

A few weeks in David said to me, "I don't think you can do business in China."

"Why?"

"Well, you don't drink alcohol."

Marilyn and I chose not to drink. We had people close to us who were alcoholics and we saw how drinking ruined their families.

I said, "You've got to explain this to me, David, I don't understand."

He said, "Well, in China they have a thing called *gānbēi*. *Gānbēi* is the Oriental toast equivalent to 'Cheers!' or more literally 'Empty your cup!' So, you sit around a big round table, and everybody salutes you. If there's twelve people around the table, each one salutes you and that means you're drinking twelve to one. They believe that you are not honest unless you get drunk, because a drunk man tells all."

I had a lot of fun bringing that back to some strait-laced Christians. Try that one on for size. You're not honest if you're not drunk. There may be some truth to that. You get people drinking and they do talk more.

So, I said, "OK, David, we're going to China, but we're going to do it different." Things like pay our invoices quickly, if they over ship an item or two we will pay them. David would basically make a statement on integrity.

I could always lighten intense negotiations. Ed Leon taught me that. Asians are very good negotiators. I had to know the Asian business mindset to be able to negotiate with them. David taught me to be tough and not to walk away from a negotiation without a good deal. If you give in too early, they don't respect you. But the Chinese love to laugh. They thought Americans were too serious. I'm serious, but I had fun with them. I brought Canadian pencils and I'd say, "You've got to sharpen your price. Here's a Canadian pencil because these Chinese pencils are too dull."

I would never hesitate to go out to dinner with them, but I told David, "You must ensure this is orchestrated. You choose the restaurant. I want to go to eat and nothing else." So very early on they learned my standards, and they thought I was unusual, but 35, 40 years later, some of those guys that drank the very heavy liquor have all kinds of health problems. They see me now as a healthy guy: "You're really in good shape."

In Taiwan there was a practice called "serving tea." Westerners call it prostitution. As business expanded through Asia in the 80s, and Taiwan became an economic power, North Americans became familiar with teahouses. In many cases, they were a way of doing business. David warned me that many Asian deals came packaged with a night in a teahouse. It was culturally acceptable for wealthy Asian business owners to have at least one mistress. Asians were perplexed when David explained that all Richard wanted in a deal was money. By the grace of God and being married to a wonderful wife, I was spared a downfall that many fall into with a lot of travel.

A prostitute is a bottomless pit; a loose woman can get you into deep trouble fast. She takes you for all you've got.
— Proverbs 23:27-28 (MSG)

On one trip we went into northern China. It took hours to get there on a train with hard wooden seats. The locomotive looked to be from the 50s. The guy seated across from me had a live chicken in a bag. I could just see the feet with the head down. We were on that train for five—maybe six—hours going into a remote part of China.

I am six foot four with shoes on and when we got off the train we caused a bit of a commotion. Some people had never seen a white person, let alone a giant. They would come up to me and laugh.

I was being picked up by a government vehicle, an Audi 8. There were Chinese flags on the corners of the car and drapes on the side windows. The Chinese government was involved in all business negotiations. I was a foreigner coming into a very high-level meeting. All I wanted to do was buy two end tables and a coffee table, the simplest form of furniture you could buy. From my experience I knew that this was a simple product to start in a new factory.

We negotiated a price for at least six hours with eighteen people. I'd never negotiated with that many people. But remember, China is all for the people. So, everybody of any consequence in that factory that had a management position was in the meeting. It was a big deal for them to meet a Western person and negotiate.

We used translators and they offered crazy prices at the beginning. They wanted Magnussen to pay what they wanted or thought they needed to make the tables. They had no concept of how to position a product to compete at retail in North America. In China, the price was the price. The leaders had no understanding of price point to sell in America. Their perspective grew out of roots of communism back in the day. China has come a long way.

We ended up not putting a deal together. Word came back a couple days later that they were shocked that we didn't buy anything from them. They had the idea that we should pay them what they wanted.

They treated David and me like royalty, hosting a big dinner at a restaurant. There was live shrimp on the tables. They would pour alcohol over them, maybe to purify them. But the shrimp were being burned and one of them jumped on my plate. I'm not a sushi lover. Cockroaches were running up and down the restaurant wall. The tablecloths were only changed once a week, and it looked like the week wasn't up. Fisheyes were a delicacy in China. I warned David that Western people don't feel comfortable eating fisheyes and things like that.

A lot of westerners would go back to Hong Kong when they were finished their day in China, because they didn't want to live in the hotels. But I wanted to experience the whole thing, and I felt it was a better statement that I was there and not some kind of arrogant person. I would eat anything that was boiled. Sometimes I had to brush my teeth with Coca-Cola. I travelled for 37 years to Asia and only felt a little ill once or twice.

When Lisa was eleven, I took her on one of my business trips to Taiwan. She showed curiosity and interest in wanting to see what I did when I was away. I warned her it was just boring business. You can guess what happens when all the suppliers learn that my eleven-year-old daughter is coming with me. Hotels get bumped up and they're nicer. Little side trips get planned in Hong Kong. Special treats just for her.

The people in Asia were so hospitable and such good hosts. McDonald's had just opened in Taiwan, and it was a big deal for corporations to cater from McDonald's. They would lay out a reception for Lisa with Big Macs and fries.

She got a feel for what international travel was like. Going through time zones, hearing people speak an entirely different language, reading signage she didn't understand. Lots of questions. It was a shorter, two-week trip in the summer so she wouldn't miss school. Lisa hung in through the entire experience. No complaints. She had a ball.

We started contracting work out of Mexico: metal tables and Mexican rough pine in occasional tables and cabinets. Kelly was about fourteen or fifteen when he came on a summertime trip with me to Tijuana to see the factories. He was right in there with me, going through all the discussions and what it's like working through a language barrier. I wanted him to get a taste of doing business in a foreign country. The food, people dynamics, and having his eyes opened to a different world. It's like taking the blinders off and broadening your appreciation for what you have.

Laura went on two mission trips. One trip was to Washington, DC where she spent time in a ghetto with her youth group. The second was a three-week group trip to Kenya and Uganda when she was fifteen. A friend from church initially invited Laura to go with her and a team called Word of Life out of New York, but she cancelled a few weeks before departure. Laura decided she would go on her own, so we drove our fifteen-year-old baby daughter to Toronto so she could fly to New York and travel with a group of forty-nine American strangers. The group did musical performances in thirty-four schools and shared with the students the love of Jesus. Laura told us on return that it was a trip of a lifetime with smells, experiences, and encounters with God she would never forget.

Laura was our picky eater so we knew there would be some meals she might not be inclined to enjoy on her trip. She managed fine with the food and with her return trip. She flew on her own out of Africa, into Detroit where she transferred to a flight to Toronto. She had no cell phone to rely on, but her fifteen-year-old mind remembered my advice: "Laura, an airport is one of the most well-labelled places. Follow the signs to your gate and the baggage claim and, if you're ever in doubt, there is a ticket counter every twenty to thirty feet, so you can just stop and ask them, and they will help you." Her first international solo trip. Can you tell I am proud of her?

All our kids were confident in tackling things their peers may have been reluctant to do. They were capable of handling things on their own. These adventures were my way of helping them be independent, see other cultures, and understand that not everybody lives like we do in Canada or the United States.

The idea behind these trips came from listening to an American pastor tell the story of his father sending him on an around the world trip when he was only sixteen. He travelled country to country, on his own, visiting missionaries. His dad threw him into the deep end to learn to trust God and become independent. And it worked. In his twenties, the pastor began to develop a global network that would grow to thousands of churches and pastors. My hope was our kids would become comfortable living and doing business in cultures and with people who were not like them but would be liked by them. The world is shrinking and advancing quickly.

Over the decades, I watched China go from dirt roads with huge potholes to superhighways. I was given a lesson in real time about a culture going from poverty and bicycles to a more Western standard of living and luxury cars. Government officials candidly shared with me that they had to make sure their citizens were doing better and better, because they couldn't afford a revolt of 1.2 billion people.

Integrity was something we were willing to pay a price to maintain. When we received shipments, sometimes the account wasn't right. A container may have one or two pieces more or maybe one piece less. Most importers will tell if they're short one or two pieces, but none of them will say, "I got two more. You've got to charge me for those two extra pieces of furniture."

So right off the bat I said, "That is standard. That's the way we're going to do it." David said, "I don't think it'll work."

I imagine some business people thought, *Magnussen is really sloppy. They're paying us for shipping too many.* That was not heard of. But that was my edge. In the big scheme of things tables weren't that expensive. But it made the statement that we're going to be honest in all our dealings. The companies learned they could rely on us to be honest and pay our bill on time. It was like a bank making payments. They were blown away.

Magnussen had a few critics suggest that we operated in Asia to simply take advantage of low-cost labor. But the reality was we gave people work for better pay, and the whole country did better. We contributed to the economy through factory jobs paying good wages. In setting up manufacturing at the beginning, we would talk about the efficiency of machinery versus labor. But the mindset there was the need to employ people so they could earn a living because they didn't have the safeguard of unemployment. In the customer care center in Vietnam, we were paying two or three times as much as local jobs.

Blessed are those who are generous, because they feed the poor.
— *Proverbs 22:9 (NLT)*

Our goal was to provide 24-hour, six-days-a-week customer care service. We set it up in Vietnam because there was a twelve-hour time difference. We brought Vietnamese workers to Canada for training. They were all university graduates who spoke English. People in our office were impressed with how gracious these young people were and by how seriously they took their training.

They were rotated around to different trainers to learn specific aspects of the job. They made handwritten notes during the day and when they came back in the morning, the information would be typed and formatted in a binder. That's the way they were trained in university. Our people were blown away by the work ethic and the commitment they had. One of Magnussen's core values was to provide a high level of Human Resources support and consideration for each individual. We wanted to raise the standard of living and help our employees become competitive with Western companies.

The ways and means of Asian countries could be a hinderance or an unexpected benefit depending on the circumstance. When I was travelling to Vietnam, I needed a visa. Back then they issued a visa that was good for the duration of a trip. My travel agent would send my passport to the liaison office in Canada, pay a couple of hundred dollars and the visa, along with the returned passport, arrived at our office a few days later. On one trip I went through Toronto International Airport, flying on Cathay Pacific to Anchorage Alaska to refuel, on to Hong Kong, and then arriving in Vietnam. Those are killer trips of about twenty-seven hours travel time. It's hard to sleep, so after arriving tired, you have to go through customs, hoping things go smoothly. At the end of one trip, the customs agent looked at my visa and then back at me.

"Visa is not valid."

I was shocked. "There must be a mistake. I paid for that visa. It must be good."

The agent spoke very little English, and I spoke no Vietnamese, but using hand signals and some broken English, he drew my attention to the date on my visa. The month and the day were reversed.

"Visa no good. You have to go back on plane."

"No, I can't. I'm here to buy a lot of furniture. I can't go back on the plane. There's some kind of mix-up."

As with any time things go sideways, I reached out to my manager in Vietnam in a bit of a panic. He assured me he would get it figured out as fast as he could. The next thing I knew, an agent was ushering me through the crowd to a line clearly marked for diplomats. When they asked for my passport and started walking away with it, I said, "Whoa, I need my passport." They were able to assure me not to worry, they would have it back to me with the official visa. I'm back on the phone to my manager. "They took my passport. You've got to track this. I can't be here without a passport."

And sure enough, they came through with my passport stamped and a new visa. Everything was fine. My manager had called a travel agent, and the only way they could get me into the country was as a diplomat. So, I was diplomat for an hour. They took me through a special kind of place of honor for diplomats. I was treated royally. What a turn of events. And I thought, *Now here's an interesting thing, my visa is not right and I'm going through as a diplomat.* That's the thing I liked about some of those countries. They figure out a way to get things done. No doubt there was a payoff or commission for some official.

The Asian venture was not without its intrigue. An office manager in one country embezzled $400,000 US. We never saw it coming. The manager came highly recommended, smart, wonderful, and with the innocence of a Sunday school teacher. They spoke very good English. Highly capable. The individual was made head of finance and accounting. We put a lot of trust in the individual and paid them an incentive to be a good company person.

Our operations manager, Chris, caught on to something, did a personal audit, and discovered the theft. He learned that the manager was buying from our suppliers, adding 10% to our price, and pocketing the profit. It looked like the deceit had gone on for two years. In Canada, we would call a lawyer, bring in HR, and lay the case out. But that wouldn't have necessarily gotten our money back nor would it have dealt with it in a way that the individual could turn around. I went to Mr. Tin, the owner of our distribution center, for advice on what to do. The office manager had worked for him and came with his blessing. He was surprised by the behavior. But he advised against the Western way.

"Meet with the office manager and lay out all the money that was embezzled. Say that there will be a period of time to pay it back. If the manager fails to make payments, we bring the police in. Nobody wants to go to a jail in our country."

We confronted the manager and there was an admission of guilt. The embezzled money was being invested in condos in Ho Chi Minh City, which was a good investment because they kept rising in value. We offered a little bit of time to think. Culturally, being guilty would be a huge embarrassment to the manager's parents and everybody around them. The manager agreed to make payments and return all the money over 18 months. During the process I received emails from the person saying that since I was a Christian where was the mercy and grace? I responded by saying we are being merciful and gracious to you because you wouldn't want to be in jail. We were paid back every dime over the stipulated period of time.

The experience was a wakeup call for us.

Our managers took an interest in the political and cultural systems of all the countries we operated in to better understand the pressures on the lives of our employees. In Taiwan, particularly, there's always been a threat that China will take over. David and I would drive along the seafront in Taiwan, and I'd ask, "Why aren't they building beautiful homes or apartments overlooking the ocean?" David answered. "That's China. No one would want to build on the beach because of the fear of China coming and invading."

The Taiwanese managed plants for us in Vietnam and China. They were good plant managers, very tough. We started importing from Taiwan (1983), then opened up the Philippines (1989), China (1990), Indonesia (1990), Singapore (1990), Malaysia (1990) and Vietnam (2000). Each new country we went into expanded our product line so we could offer furniture made from stone, glass and metal, as well as wood. Over time we went into twenty markets including the Middle East, New Zealand, Germany, and Korea.

Every country was a little different and it sometimes took us a while to understand the rules of local business. Magnussen was the first Canadian furniture company to be in Vietnam. We opened an office with about ten employees and immediately ran into a culture problem. The Vietnamese did not realize that we were paying some people more money for more responsibility. They were used to a system where everybody was paid the same amount. The employees were very upset but, over time, coaching helped them adjust. Every employee was a university graduate. Their work ethic was incredible. No complaining.

Singapore was interesting. The manager of the factory we worked with was a devout Buddhist. He was having quality problems. So, he hired a priest to come in, and had to pay $10,000 for a "quality" god. They put the idol at the end of the production line and changed all the doors to face the east. It was a 500,000 square foot plant. The priest put baby goats in the field next to them. That's what the priest told them would increase quality.

When we were first importing furniture from Taiwan, we had to overcome the "Made in China" reputation. When Taiwan started exporting furniture, Canadians considered it junk. The reason was there was a guy in California who was shipping all his defective furniture to Western Canada, and you could buy it cheap. Of course, you have to stamp the country of origin on the product. The veneer started to crack a bit and they would ship that up to Canada and just basically give it away. The veneer cracked because of poor quality control in Taiwan.

In a humid climate, which Taiwan is, you have to be very careful. If there's excess moisture in the wood, it'll come out in dry climates and then it'll crack. That was a foundational thing that we had to overcome. We were overly scrupulous in making sure that our manager always had a moisture meter. He would check the wood coming out of the kilns, and he would check on the assembly lines. When the tabletops were being assembled to the frames and aprons, we had to insure it wasn't out there too long collecting moisture. It's like a sponge at that point because there's no sealer on it. We built control rooms where we had heat and humidity controlled by dehumidification. When the product was waiting to go on the finishing line, it would stay in the control room to make sure there was no moisture on the veneer.

Magnussen became one of the top Canadian trading partners with China in the furniture industry, totaling over 7,600 shipments a year. China was ripe for North American-branded products. We sold Magnussen Home brand furniture to the local China market. Chinese loved American brands even if they were made in China.

New markets were also opening to sell Magnussen Home brand furniture in the Middle East, New Zealand, Germany and Korea.

I owe any success to my dad. I took him on one trip to Taiwan and showed him the factories. He passed away in 1986 before he got to see how we grew to all the categories of furniture from the little company he started.

One thing my dad and I had in common was love for our kids. He was a great grandpa to all of his six grandkids. My dad wasn't present at my sports events when I was a teen. No fault on him, that wasn't how he was raised. I wanted to instill a new set of values as our kids grew up so that they could carry them forward into their future families

All three of our kids played school sports. Kelly's were football and basketball, and Lisa and Laura played volleyball. Kelly was a great athlete and went to Trinity Western in BC to play basketball. In high school he transferred out of the school his sisters attended because they didn't have a football team. He moved over to Grand River Collegiate.

It was rare for me not to be at their games. The only times I missed were when I was out of the country. It wasn't unusual to be in Asia for three weeks at a time, which left Marilyn parenting on her own. Marilyn and I made the decision that she would stay at home because that was her passion. She's a great mother and an unbelievable Nana. She covered the home front and allowed me to travel and do what was necessary to grow the business. We knew I was missing a lot of the kids' growing up, so Marilyn did everything she could to keep us all connected. I track the same way with our grandkids, trying to get to as many of their volleyball games, equestrian events, soccer matches, and golf games as possible.

International phone calls were expensive, around $4.00 a minute. I tried to call frequently. Marilyn would rush the kids to the phone and remind them they couldn't talk long but tell Dad how your day went. It wasn't clear reception, and the calls were over all too quickly, but we did what it took to maintain contact.

When I came home from a trip, I got the footnotes of what was going on in our three children's lives. Marilyn kept track of what each child did at school or church or in sports while I was away. She would brief me.

Saturday was yard work in the morning and then I would have a special time with the kids at lunch at Wendy's, their favorite fast-food place. Over burgers and fries I would casually weave Marilyn's information into our date times.

If I needed to pick up something at the hardware store, I'd take Lisa or Laura and we'd turn it into a date. We'd do what we had to and then go to Wendy's. We sat and talked and found out about how things were going in life. I loved those times together.

Later in life I asked the kids if they thought I wasn't there for them and they said, "No, you were always on top of everything." They hadn't put it together that their mother and I were working as a team. That's the only way I was able to go on business and work long, long hours. Marilyn was a pillar in our home. It was a perfect partnership. We balanced each other and still do. We just signed a contract for another 50 years of marriage.

Chapter 12, International Dreams

Are you intrigued by the idea of running a business that's not just about profits but also respects employees and contributes to societal good? The effects of ethical business practices go beyond a company's internal environment. The ethical operation of your business is directly tied to profitability in both the short and long term. More customers now choose to support ethical brands that provide equal employment, fair wages, a transparent supply chain, and measurable environmental efforts. These companies are doing it right.

- In what ways does your life and business reflect ethical values and practices?
- Are there areas in your operation where you could improve on "doing it right"?

13

ANCHORED BY HOPE

MY PARENTS PURCHASED LAKEFRONT PROPERTY AT SAUBLE Beach on Lake Huron to build a cottage where many of my childhood memories were formed.

Sauble is a popular, thirteen-mile beach, and we thought it was the best beach in Ontario. Some might challenge that, but we loved it. The lot Dad purchased was one that nobody wanted because it had a stream running through it and wasn't all that big, which dissuaded buyers who wanted to build a cottage. But my dad saw things others didn't. To my dad, that was the most attractive lot to have because of the stream running through it. He and I are built the same way. We see possibility where others see liability.

Dad hired framers and carpenters, but he did all the stonework. That was his hobby. He positioned his cottage very high on the property because he had the foresight to note that the sand dunes were building up. His neighbor wasn't happy, but Dad picked a good spot to build. Decades later, his cottage still sits above the sand dunes overlooking Lake Huron with a gorgeous view of beautiful summer sunsets. He built a nice little pond with a toy sailboat anchored in it. No one would go by his cottage without stopping and looking at the landscaping.

Dad had a catamaran sailboat that we could pull right up on the beach. We boated a lot together. I certainly remember my heart beating a bit faster during my first sailing experience. But I learned to love the thrill of being on the open water, sun on my face, and sails catching the breeze. You could see for miles. Lake Huron has remarkably blue water and it is considered among the cleanest of the Great Lakes.

His catamaran was the first of its kind on our beach. It had a wooden deck, taller mast, and was fast. Dad and I learned together how to sail it. Just the two of us would go out as my mother was not much for sailing because she wasn't a swimmer. By the time I was around sixteen, I had become pretty proficient at it. My dad wouldn't be at the cottage all the time so I would take it out by myself.

The rougher the weather the more I loved going out. I was comfortable in storm winds. With the wind up I could get extra speed. On days like that the boat would tip sideways to the water. The technical term is heeling. When a sailboat catches the wind, it will heel or lean over at an angle. The wind pressure on the sails forces the boat to a sideway angle. That can feel unstable, especially if you're not really into sailing. For a beginner, heeling over can be intimidating. If you didn't know better, you'd be convinced the boat was going to flip over at any moment. I've seen a few white faces on their first sailing trip.

I loved taking our boat to the limit and beyond, doing stunts and catching some air. On one particular afternoon, so I was told, I had some spectators. I probably gave the beach lovers a good show with the stunts. I wasn't trying to show off. I just loved the exhilarating feeling of being right at the very brink of the thing.

And then the day came when I went over the brink.

When the boat flipped and spilled me under the water, I didn't panic when I came to the surface. My dad had trained me how to right the boat for an occasion just like this. However, the problem that day was that the breeze was blowing offshore, and I was headed towards Michigan. Someone on shore must have called the OPP, which was a good idea because I was drifting further and further away.

The police arrived, picked me up, and towed me in. I even made the newspaper. The news media from nearby Owen Sound must have been monitoring the police scanner. They showed up and took pictures. There must be a photo album somewhere. That was the only time I flipped a sailboat, although we did come close a few other times.

By the time the grandkids came along, Dad had purchased a 17-foot sailboat. It wasn't that big, but he'd pack my sister's sons and our kids onboard, and they'd sail up the coast, pretending they were pirates. They have fond memories of those adventures that often surface at family get-togethers.

Years later, I was looking to buy a sailboat. I found a locally owned 36-footer. My dad said, "You know what, you should ask the guy to take you sailing. And if you don't buy it, you just pay for the hours he had you out." That's a good idea, Dad.

We went out and it was a good, windy day. A bit too windy for Marilyn. She had Laura on her chest in one of those baby carriers. It was probably a 25-knot wind that day, which was not unusual for the Bay. The wind caught the sail and the boat started to heel. I loved the feeling, but for a mom with her three kids there was a whole different reaction.

Things did not go well with Marilyn. She was upset. Laura was screaming. Lisa was nervous. Kelly was pretty good. He was enjoying it like I was, but it was a very clear picture we weren't buying that sailboat. Marilyn asked to get off at Big Bay. The owner's wife picked her up because she was so terrified. My dad, Kelly, and I sailed back with the owner. It was a great day for us.

I wanted Marilyn to enjoy the water and, after her misadventures with sailing, we bought a 43-foot powerboat. Now that was a much better choice of craft. Marilyn took swimming lessons so she would have more confidence on the water. She came a long way from fear of the water to swimming lessons. I really respect her for trying to have adventures with me.

Weekends in the summer were big for our family. We spent them on the water. I would leave work early on Thursdays. Marilyn had the car packed. Once the kids got home from school, we were off to the marina where our boat was docked.

As soon as we boarded, we put on Richard Clayderman's music. Piano only. When that music was played it meant we were relaxing on the boat. Our weekend had started. Marilyn especially loved it because the kids were always around us. It was very much family time. They had friends and they'd be on and off the boat, using the water equipment or visiting on another boat. But they were close.

On Friday morning we'd go out, find a little cove, and set the anchor.

Setting an anchor is more than just dropping it over the side. You let your anchor down to the bottom. Then you have to back your boat off to what they call a scope. An anchor is very small compared to the weight of the boat. The greater the scope, the stronger the hold. You must back the boat up so that that anchor can dig into the lakebed. There are different anchors suited to different types of lakebeds. You want to choose the right anchor for your conditions.

The way other boaters set their anchor would tell me who may be bumping into my boat. Sometimes we moved if the predominant wind was blowing our way because I could count on a boat with a poorly set anchor bumping against us. I would look at the forecast and see if the wind was going to change overnight and put us at risk. If necessary, I would move in the night. In the morning, the boat owners around us wondered why we weren't there.

The boat was a wonderful place to entertain friends. Three staterooms allowed us to have people on the boat with us. Good food and lots of it was always a feature. We had a barbecue on board and a dishwasher, so clean-up was quick and easy. We had lots of fun windsurfing and water skiing behind the dingy. These leisurely weekends afforded time to relax and talk and sometimes I opened discussions with our guests over interesting stories or subjects from the Bible.

One weekend we had invited a Jewish couple. There are a lot of Jewish people in the furniture business who I consider friends. Our friend sounded tentative with the thought of a Bible study. She shared that she had always been taught that Christians didn't like Jews because Jews killed Jesus. I said, "Well, wait a minute. Jesus was Jewish and we have been taught that Jews are God's chosen people. So, I don't believe what you think I believe."

That was a helpful perspective for her. And the discussion helped me understand how Jews think.

On Saturday we'd weigh anchor and cruise around the bay. Sometimes we'd anchor near an island, take a smaller tender boat ashore, and go on a hike. Saturday evening, we typically would dock at the marina and go back to the city to attend church on Sunday morning. We didn't want our kids to think that church was secondary to anything else. The kids didn't think much about it other than that's the way it was.

My parents were in their late 60s when they bought a place in Venice, Florida. A double wide trailer in a nice community. They made the purchase with their family in mind. The five of us would go south in the winter and enjoy the sun with Grandpa and Grandma. It was great for our kids, and Dad experienced his own second childhood.

Dad discovered an untapped passion for Disney World in his 70s. His first visit to the amusement park ignited a love for the world of make-believe. Every day he would be at the front of the line when the gates opened. With the abandon of a child, he literally ran to the attractions. He couldn't get enough of the Tom Sawyer ride, Frontier Adventure, and taking trips on the river of Mark Twain. Dad was enthralled with how Disney did shows so well. It never grew old for him. I understood what he felt, but where I might have been a level six, he was at level eleven. Even my father-in-law couldn't get over how Dad was such a big fan of Disney World.

I received my dad's beach area lots in an inheritance and, not long after, a real estate agent inquired about purchasing two of them. I told him if he found me some lakefront lots on Georgian Bay that had some privacy, I would consider selling two lots to him. He called me a few weeks later. "Richard, I've got the lots for you. Put an offer in, pay full price and no conditions."

I asked, "What's the price?"

"It's just under forty acres and it's $150,000 for the lot. Put no conditions on other than you get to see it within three days."

"I should negotiate a little bit, right?"

"Richard, trust me. Just go full price."

I did trust him because he knew his business, and I made the offer at full price. The property was about a half an hour away from my dad's cottage. When I saw it, I wondered what was wrong with it, because it certainly looked too good to be true for that price.

The agent explained that the property was under the jurisdiction of the Niagara Escarpment Authority. The Niagara Escarpment is a rock formation that extends from Niagara Falls up to northern Ontario and is heavily protected as a natural resource.

I asked if the problem was that they wouldn't let property owners build?

"No, you can build a home, a summer home or whatever you want." However, there was a rigorous approval process to do any building and that dissuaded impatient potential owners.

It was an amazing piece of land and $150,000 was a very good price, even in 1986. Within a year someone offered me half a million for it. We purchased the 1300 feet of waterfront between Wiarton and Owen Sound at Colpoy's Bay, which is a part of Georgian Bay. The Bay is named after Sir John Colpoy, who was an Admiral in the British Navy during the early 1800s.

Turns out the owner had quite a bit of property, but he didn't like the bureaucracy. Too many hoops to jump through for him. In his frustration, he put the land on the market for his price. He didn't even take the time to appreciate what it was worth. His father had published a book about the history of that area along Georgian Bay. I have a copy of the book. Those are interesting stories about the people who inhabited this area two hundred years ago.

I felt a bit apprehensive when I went to get approvals, but I discovered that the Niagara Escarpment Authority wanted what I wanted. They didn't want to see clear cutting, and they didn't want the land damaged. My plans exactly.

I'm the visionary, and when I bought the land, I wanted to build my dream as soon as the title transferred to me. But Marilyn said we should wait. The kids were young. The business was taking most of my energy. We wouldn't have time to care for the business and our home and cottage. It took me ten years of patiently sitting on the property. But she was right.

We had to first put a road in to access the land, and then we broke ground in March of 1997. Marilyn and I were engaged in the entire process. We went to Cape Cod to source out design ideas. I took over 200 pictures of features we liked about the styles. Our cottage is very Cape Cod. There was a lot of thoughtful planning that went into the layout and design. We wanted the sun to come into our little morning room where we would have coffee. There was a myriad of similar details. We took a lot of pleasure and pride in making it feel purposeful and beautiful. After twenty years we completely renovated the cottage but kept the three main structures.

I'm very big into maintenance. People who see the cottage for the first time think it's new. An annual coat of fresh paint where there is wear does wonders. That's how we treat all our properties. I have painters come in every year at the cottage, our condo in Waterloo, and our home in Florida. We get the cottage painted usually in March or April, so it feels like new when we come in for the summer. It is quite pristine. I learned the habit of taking good care of our things from my wife. I was such a slob when we got married, but she taught me well.

The builders, Dale and Carolyn, owners of Traditions, and our interior designer, Silvana Lewis, had the cottage all finished just before Christmas, but they dissuaded us from coming around until they could ready it for a reveal for our whole family. It was very nice of them to put up a Christmas tree and decorate the entire place for Christmas. We went wild when we saw it. It looked like it could be on the cover of a design magazine. There is a main cottage, and a coach house, which has a special garage down below. It includes a gym with my office above. A boathouse by the water accommodates a guest suite on the second level.

Lisa got married in '95 and Kelly got married in '97. Lisa, Kelly, their spouses, and Laura got to choose their bedrooms and to this day when they visit, those are the bedrooms they sleep in.

We've added more bedrooms as the family has grown. Marilyn and I have the main suite. It's the only home that we've kept for all these years. We've moved around here, there, and everywhere, but the cottage we've enjoyed now for 26 years.

When we landscaped the property, we used flagstones as a walkway. I don't remember where the idea came from, but we wanted to see if we could have words carved on some of the flagstones. So I went to a local business that engraves gravestones and they were more than happy to help me out.

There are nine flagstones. Each is engraved with one word.

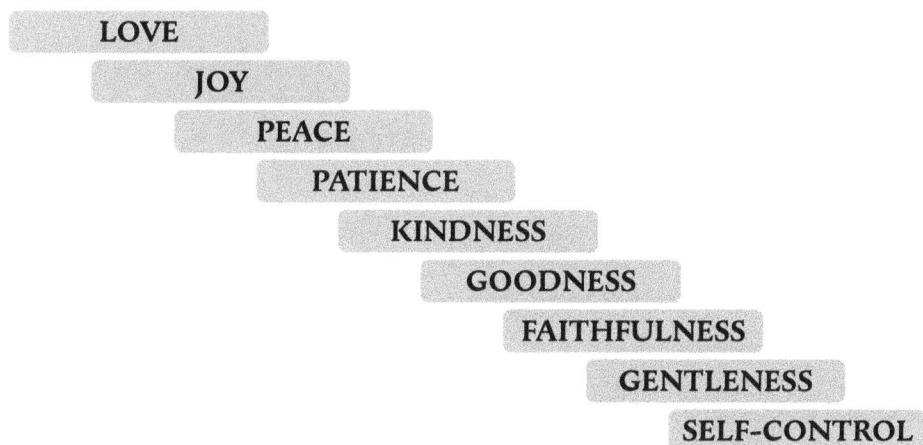

Repairmen who would do work on the cottage often asked if we got the idea out of a Martha Stewart magazine. No, the words come from the Bible.

The words are a list of some of the characteristics of a follower of Jesus. They are called "the fruit of the Spirit" in the New Testament book of Galatians, chapter 5, verses 22 and 23. Whenever guests used the cottage they always commented on the layout.

The stones made for great teaching moments. I would send my grandkids out when they needed to be working on different issues. We made a game of it. "Let's find the fruit of the Spirit that you need the most right now and go stand on that rock." We would say a little prayer.

Funny how patience was the most popular. Sometimes I had to stand on a stone.

We had a few sailboats, including a Trimaran. That was fun. It consisted of a main hull and two hydro foils which looked like metal wings or skis. It was fast. When it got up to a certain speed, we put down the foils and the boat would lift and ski on the foils with no water resistance from the hull. Did I say I love the feeling of speed? We did a lot of sailing, although none of the grandkids have caught my enthusiasm yet.

When the grandkids were little, I would take them out on our 28-foot twin engine. We would pack a lunch, find a calm spot to anchor, and swim off the back of the boat. Sometimes it'd be just me and the grandkids, which could be five or six of them. But when they were very young, I always wanted one of the other adults to come along. That would usually be Laura. She was the most interested in learning how to operate a power boat. On one boating adventure, Laura and I towed a boat back to shore that had ran out of fuel.

Marilyn is very good at setting traditions. Every weekend, we had to boat up to Big Bay and go to the general store. They served the best homemade ice cream, and the scoops were generous. It was worth the little wait to line up for the delicious taste. It's just a short walk to the shore and pier to take in the view of the Bay and the islands while you enjoy the scrumptious ice cream. Their flavors changed frequently, often with seasonal choices, like pumpkin pie on the menu for Thanksgiving weekend. The kids are all adults now, but when we're at the cottage for a weekend, we have to go to Big Bay and have a homemade ice cream cone.

One time we were going to arrive maybe five minutes after closing time. We called ahead and said, "There's fourteen of us." They said, "Don't come. We won't serve you. We're closing." We all laughed. "OK, five minutes isn't worth waiting to serve fourteen customers?"

Another family tradition is Tim Horton's in the mornings on the dock. Now we're buying Tim Horton's for fourteen people early in the morning and bringing it back. Everybody sits on the dock. It's tradition.

There are so many cottage memories for our kids and our grandchildren. That's all they've known. The grandkids came to the cottage every summer, their whole lives. And we used to have Christmas there too, until we bought our property in Florida.

The grandkids say, "Nana and Papa, you won't ever sell the cottage, will you?" And Marilyn says, "Well, I can't promise that. You know, everything has its time. We all love the cottage, but I don't know what's ahead." She would tease. "I don't know if we can look after it. It's a huge place."

"But don't sell it, Nana."

"Well, you know, you all live down in Carolina. It'll just go to pot and look terrible if nobody is there to look after and live in it. We'll see what God has for us. You know, God always gives us beautiful homes, so don't worry about it."

We have been happy to share the cottage with friends and guests. Pastor Ken used it for weekend meetings with the elders from our church. In February 2022 he used it as a retreat center for a group of thirteen pastors that he was mentoring. They were sleeping on the floor and in different places for beds, but they raved about their experience.

We love to further God's work through generously giving what we have been given.

My Dad lived a full life, and he was full of life.

You know those little buzzers that you put in your hand and when you shake someone's hand it goes buzz? Sunday mornings, he would be in the back of the church when everybody's leaving, and he would shake hands with someone, and they would squeak. My mother was always so embarrassed, but that was my dad. He wanted to get a rise out of people and have some fun. He was one of a kind. That's part of why, at nineteen, he chose to immigrate away from his family, even when he was offered a free ride to study at the next level of cabinetry in Germany. He was his own man. That's what gave him the strength to go to a foreign land, speaking no English. He was one of six kids, and he was the only one that chose to go to Canada. He broke the mold.

In his later years, Dad developed glaucoma. We knew that he was going to have to give up driving at some point. That would have been very hard for him. Dad was independent. He was building a retaining wall in November. Out in the snow and rain. He got the flu. It was rare for my dad to be sick. If he was sick, he never went to the doctor, but this time he was admitted to hospital. Lisa and I went to see him, and he did not look good. He was very white and pasty. He was supposed to come home the next day. That morning at 3:00, I got a call from my mom. Dad had passed. I was shocked. He had developed a blood clot and died suddenly in the hospital. He was 78.

Early the next morning, the kids found me grieving in our family room.

My mom died at 96. Some people get grumpy when they get old. I want to be like my mom. She loved everybody and she told them. If you met her for two minutes she would say, "I love you because of Jesus." I would visit her at the seniors' home where she lived. If there was an aide in her room, she'd pull me over and introduce me to this person. She would say, "This man takes such good care of me." And she would build him up. "I love him because of Jesus."

Sometimes care workers are overworked and can't respond to every request, but my mom got anything she wanted. They loved her. Why? Because she showed them love and she would brag about them. It was a little embarrassing for me because I'd come for a visit, and she'd introduce me. She'd tell them how great I was. I'd say, "Mom, don't you remember when I threw a dart at my sister, Alice, because I didn't get my TV selection." Mom would say, "That was a mistake. You didn't mean to hit her in the foot with a dart." She couldn't be convinced that I wasn't her Golden Boy.

Mom kept all her faculties right till the end. The doctors told us that she could live another lifetime with her heart. It was her other organs that started shutting down. My sister was very faithful to my mom, taking care of her needs. Alice and I were both there with her in her final earthly hour. She was at peace. We watched her breathing stop and thought she was gone. Then all of a sudden she took a big deep breath. Moments later she breathed her last. I saw how death comes. Her death took some of the fear away because my mom showed us how.

It was about four in the morning on a Thanksgiving weekend. Marilyn was at the cottage because we had guests. After Mom passed, I drove to the cottage and arrived around 7:00 am. Marilyn was sleeping, so I went to the loft to be by myself. As soon as Marilyn woke up, she sent me an e-mail. "Where are you and how is Mom?" I replied, "She passed and I'm in the loft." Marilyn came up and we talked about Mom. She was a sweet, sweet lady. Sweeter as she got older.

Laura says, "I've only seen my dad cry twice. My first recollection was when my grandpa died. I was seven. My parents had two reclining chairs in our family room. One was always my mom's, one was always my dad's. And Dad was sitting in my mom's chair and he was crying. His dad had died. I'd never seen him cry in my life. And then I don't think I've ever seen him cry since then, until my grandma died in 2011. I remember he drove to the cottage from the hospital, and he was sitting upstairs, crying. My grandma was a remarkable woman."

I learned to set anchor from my dad. His and my mom's faith in Jesus were their anchors of hope. I am grateful for the grounding they gave me, and I have been able to pass on to my family.

Chapter 13, Anchored By Hope

Strategic anchors provide a clear and coherent set of principles that guide a business's strategic choices and decisions. This is the real guts of a strategy for success and guides the choices made and actions pursued. Personal convictions provide a clear and coherent set of principles that guide your life choices and decisions. Convictions are the real guts of a strategy for a successful life, family, and career.

- What convictions have created success for you to date?
- What have been your inherent sources of success?
- What are your business's unique strengths?

14

THE CHOSEN

I AM A COMMITTED FOLLOWER OF JESUS, BUT I DON'T LIKE all things Christian.

When the online series, *The Chosen*, first released, I watched a few episodes, but they didn't grab my attention. When COVID sent us to our rooms, friends encouraged me to give the series another try, so Marilyn and I started to binge watch. It only took a few episodes before we were hooked, turning off the TV only because it was time for bed. We completed the first two seasons and then followed each episode as season three was released. Our experiences with the series might be like your experiences with the Jesus of western Christianity. If your first encounter with Christianity left you less than impressed, giving God a second chance may be just what you need.

I love the portrayal of what I think would be the real Jesus. It's not the polished production like a lot of movies trying to portray Bible times. The producers frame the story as a street-level view of people who encountered Jesus. The camera work tries to make it look like a documentary. The episodes aren't preachy. No sermons. Simply good storytelling. I forget that the disciples were nomads and women like Mary Magdalene were with the original twelve. We are limited with a Western mindset of who Jesus is, how he looked, and what a faith community should be like. We think Sundays, church, coffee, musicians, choir, PowerPoint slides, and preaching. Christianity is much bigger than evangelicals and Republicans. The reality of Jesus is far from that.

Issues that dog the modern Christian church get their fair share of attention in *The Chosen*. Poverty is a constant reality for the disciples and most people they meet. Multiple episodes focus on the tension between the Jews and Samaritans, with Jesus calling out his followers for their own prejudices. Throughout the show, as in the Bible, Jesus embraces people who are sick, disabled, and outcast, despite his disciples' clear discomfort with his actions. At the same time, the disciples grapple with their own issues: money problems, relationship concerns, jealousy and competitiveness among the group.

I've recommended the series to my friends. If you haven't seen an episode, watch one and please, let me know what you think. Contact me at www.siretona.com/goingbig.

I'm not much for books, but I did join over fifty million people who read *The Purpose Driven Life: What on Earth Am I Here For* by Rick Warren. It's one of the bestselling nonfiction books in publishing history.

Rick and his wife, Kay, founded Saddleback Church in Orange County, California, and he is considered America's pastor. He even gave the public address at a presidential inauguration. I heard Rick in person when our team of elders from Creekside Church attended one of his conferences.

The first sentence of *The Purpose Driven Life* sets the tone in the book, "It's not about you," and the remainder of the chapter goes on to explain how the quest for personal fulfillment, satisfaction, and meaning can only be found in understanding and doing what God placed you on Earth to do.

A life devoted to things is a dead life, a stump; a God-shaped life is a flourishing tree.
— Proverbs 11:28 (MSG)

Our family owes a lot to Rick Warren.

My youngest daughter, Laura, met her husband, Josh, at a gym. He was a personal trainer, and she was working out with another trainer. Josh couldn't take his eyes off her, so he asked the gym owners if they knew Laura, and was she dating anyone?

They had a couple of dates, and she really liked him, but it became clear they were on different paths. Laura's faith was the foundation of her values and

Josh had no experience with faith in Jesus or reading the Bible. She explained a few things to him, and he was open to what she said, but it was all new to him. Laura gave him a copy of *The Purpose Driven Life* and said the book would help him understand where she was coming from. Would he be willing to read it? Josh is a sincere guy. He went through the book, cover to cover.

About sixty pages in, the author invites readers to believe that God made you for a purpose, that you were created to live forever, that God chose you to have a relationship with Jesus who gave his life on the cross, and to receive Jesus as your Lord and Savior. "Wherever you are reading this, I invite you to bow your head and quietly whisper this prayer.

"*Jesus. I believe in you and receive you.*

"I urge you to tell someone about it."

Josh set up a date with Laura and told her he read the book and prayed the prayer in the book. Josh has a quiet personality and he's not inclined to emotion, but she could tell from his tone that something had shifted in his life. He accepted an invitation to come with her to Creekside that Sunday. To me it all seemed a bit convenient. You know, no faith and now he has faith and wants to go to church with my baby girl. Josh appreciated Ken Taylor's message that Sunday and took in everything like a sponge. People who knew our family soon became accustomed to seeing him regularly beside Laura at church and we got used to him in our home. Josh signed up as a volunteer in a program, and shortly after became the leader of the program.

It was no surprise the next year that he asked to have a conversation with Marilyn and me when we were at the cottage. His old-fashioned formality certainly impressed Marilyn. Josh asked for our blessing to marry Laura. We had an enjoyable couple of hours talking about spiritual things, careers, and married life. Our kids all knew what was happening, so Kelly teased us later about grilling Josh in his job interview. Planning Laura's wedding was different from her siblings.

Our house was the hangout for Kelly and Lisa's friends. They went to the same school and shared a lot of friends so when Kelly invited his friends over, Lisa would have some of her friends over. Weekend evenings were filled with lots of laughter, talking, and eating all our food. We were happy that they were there and glad to keep the food coming. Nathan was one of Kelly's friends. His dad was my best man at our wedding.

One night the group was hanging out, and Marilyn asked me, "Do you notice the way Lisa laughs when she's talking to Nathan?" No, I didn't. Marilyn said, "There's a little laugh she has that tells me that she really likes Nathan. Watch the next time they're here and see if you see it."

Before we knew it, Kelly, Nathan, and Lisa were going out together. Why would you take your younger sister with you? I should have seen what was coming.

Lisa's first date with Nathan was something else. She was my baby girl, but when she came down the stairs, she had grown fifteen years older from earlier that day. Oh, my goodness. She had a new haircut. Her skirt was short enough for Marilyn to caution, "Lisa, you can't go out like that."

Our kids couldn't date till they turned sixteen. I was fussy about the guys our girls dated. They had to pass The Richard Test. When I was working in Asia and Laura had a date, Kelly covered for me. He interviewed the guy coming to pick up Laura. And he was rough on him, which embarrassed his sister. He made sure he knew where they were going and when they'd be home. I put him in charge because that was totally Kelly.

When Lisa and Nathan got engaged, Marilyn and Lisa took time to work on a detailed wedding plan. However, Lisa and Nathan broke up, cancelling the wedding plans. They were engaged in 1994, then in 1995 they got engaged again and wanted to get married in August, which was just two months away, hold the ceremony in our front yard and the reception in the backyard. Marilyn and I advised them that allowing more time to prepare was important for them, not just for a wedding day but for their marriage. They were so disappointed. They thought they could get married in two months and just have a homestyle wedding. They went over to Nathan's parents' home, and they said the same thing, wanting to insure they were stable in their relationship. Lisa and Nathan took the wisdom of our loving counsel.

Lisa is a detailed person. Her wedding was going to be something else. Go big or go home. She is totally my girl. When the time came for planning the wedding, Lisa and Marilyn worked very closely. I think they had a 26-page manual, detailing everything, including when the bridesmaids could take a bathroom break.

Lisa was my first daughter, and she was my first child to get married. I didn't realize how overwhelming that would be. On their wedding day, it hit me that I had to give my daughter away to her husband. I never get a headache, but I had one that day. Marilyn says I turned white as a sheet. She thought I was going to pass out in the church lobby. "You look dreadful." I don't know how to describe my reaction other than it all seemed so final.

Kelly and Kim's wedding was a lot less formal because they like casual and they like the outdoors. Their ceremony was in the garden of a countryside bed and breakfast. The weather was forecast to be perfect, and then a huge rain cloud appeared, interrupting the proceedings. The wedding party and the guests scurried into the tent that was going to be used for the reception and turned it into the place to hold the service.

Planning Laura's wedding to Josh was different than her siblings' weddings. With Lisa, Marilyn was her right-hand person. With Kelly, the mom steps back when it's her son, and the daughter and her mom set the course. Laura was completely independent. "I know what I want. I'll look after it." And she did. She looked after everything.

Her budget was way over the top. The flowers were over the top. Everything was over the top, but it was sponsored by Lisa's encouragement. Lisa was my counsel. She said, "Dad, just enjoy it. It's the last one." Laura wanted to get her wedding dress in New York City, so off she went with her mom. For the final fitting, Marilyn, Laura, and all her bridesmaids went to NYC. A lot of my frequent flyer points were used. They had a ball.

Marilyn wanted Laura's guests to enjoy wonderful music at the wedding, and Marilyn didn't see any music in the ceremony schedule. That was a problem. Laura kept saying, "No music. That's just the way I want it." And Marilyn came to me all flustered and said she couldn't understand Laura. No music. That wasn't like Laura. She loved music. Laura went to Rockway, a Mennonite private school, and they were huge on music. She was in the choir. I would say, "Marilyn, it's not your wedding, it's hers. You know that."

Marilyn went to the wedding ceremony thinking, *OK, we'll see what it is without music.* Laura planned everything beautifully. A five-piece orchestra played while the guests arrived. That was good music!

Laura and I walked down the aisle as the orchestra played. I sat beside Marilyn for the rest of the ceremony. The mother of the bride seemed content.

Suddenly, angelic music came from on high.

The sound took our breath away, it was so beautiful. A choir from Laura's old school, Rockway, was quietly waiting at the back of the church in a choir loft. No one had noticed them. They started to sing softly with voices that sounded heavenly. The acoustics in the old church that Laura had chosen were incredible. This was Laura's little surprise for her mother. And was Marilyn surprised! Very pleasantly surprised. This is where Laura is like her mother. She's a super planner. She wanted to make it wonderful for her mom. Laura, you love taking your mom to the edge. That was one for Laura Lee.

Ken Taylor officiated the weddings for all our kids. Pastor Ken was with them from the nursery to the marriage altar. He was like family. We were fortunate to have a pastor like him. There was one part of his wedding ceremonies that we especially loved. He used a triangle to illustrate how to have a strong marriage. God is at the top of the triangle and the husband and wife are in the corners on the bottom. The closer the couple gets to God, the closer they were to each other.

In a world where many couples say I do and then they don't, we worked and prayed for our children to have a happily ever after with their chosen ones.

Chapter 14, The Chosen

God made you for a purpose. People with a strong sense of purpose tend to live longer, have healthier hearts, and are more psychologically resilient. Leading a purpose-driven life means aligning your actions, choices, and goals with a sense of meaning and personal mission. It involves identifying and pursuing what truly matters to you, contributing to something larger than yourself, and finding fulfillment in the process. There are three basic questions in life:

- Why am I alive?
- Does my life matter?
- What is my purpose?
- Write down in a paragraph or a single sentence, what your purpose is and what you will do with the rest of your life.

15

GO BIG

MY FRIENDS SAY I KNOW HOW TO GET STUFF DONE. FIND-A-way-or-make-a-way Magnussen. Do something right or don't do it at all. And do good.

Doing good is good for the soul.

Steve was a regular at our church going on about twenty years. He was a graduate of the University of Waterloo and was at church every Sunday in his wheelchair with a smile on his face and a positive attitude. His approach to life made him likeable. One night at his small group meeting of people from the church, Pastor Ken told them that he thought Steve could use some help to fix up his apartment. "If our whole group volunteered, we could do some good work in a day or two."

A few days later Ken called me to go over to Steve's apartment to size up what they would be dealing with. Ken says, "Let's see if the place could use some paint." I took one look inside Steve's apartment and quietly said to Ken, "We've gotta gut this place."

The carpet looked like it had never been shampooed and Steve had lived there for over two decades. The grime on the windows testified they hadn't been washed in twenty years. The appliances and fixtures were well past their best before dates. We soon discovered that Steve never wants to put anybody out. Not even family members, let alone friends. I had a little conversation with him.

"Steve, you understand the concept that it's much more blessed to give than receive? There are a lot of people who want to give to you, so you don't want to take their blessing away."

Steve said, "I understand that, but there's so many other people with needs." Ken and I looked at each other. We didn't know too many people who had more needs than Steve did.

"We love you, Steve. There are lots of people at Creekside who love you. So, if you give us permission, we'd like to get a group together and do some work on your apartment. OK?" I'm not sure if Steve knew what I had in mind, but he said yes.

On the drive back I explained to Ken the scope of the project and how we'd need a lot of people and coordination. Steve would have to be out of his apartment while we gutted it so we couldn't take long, probably a week at most. Ken drew in a breath, "A week?" Like I was crazy or something.

The extent of my plan would need the approval of the building owners. Steve was in a government subsidized unit and owners of buildings like these were never happy for tenants to fix up their unit. They would rather have a subsidized renter move out so they could rent the apartment for $1,800 to $2,000 a month. I set up a meeting with the building supervisor and explained the scope of the plan. He said he would have to get the regional manager involved. The regional manager said he would have to go up to corporate, because they didn't want just anybody messing around in their apartments. They had their own crews.

I was pleasantly surprised when the regional manager called me back to set up a meeting. I suggested we meet at Steve's apartment so I could show him what I was talking about. After explaining the extent of the plan, we moved the meeting to the sidewalk outside Steve's building. He was a man of few words, but at the end of our discussion, he said, "You're a part of Creekside, right? My wife was baptized there two years ago." I wasn't expecting that. It was a cool story. And I think that might have played into getting the approval. He reported back and said, "You can do whatever you want." That was a big, big deal.

About thirty people from Creekside's small groups rallied to the call. We arranged temporary accommodations for Steve for a week and got started. We told our team this would be our Creekside Extreme Home Makeover edition.

We tore out the kitchen cabinets, threw out the trim, ripped up the old carpet, took down the light fixtures, discarded all the weathered blinds, washed and patched the walls, readying them for a couple of new coats of paint. Tim and Ken from my small group brought their pick-up trucks and hauled 1800 pounds of materials removed from the apartment. Marilyn and Carol Taylor rolled up their sleeves, all in and ready to paint. Marilyn said, "Teach me how to cut in, Ken." They worked together on painting the new baseboards. She really enjoyed it because there was a lot of community with people.

On day one, our work got the attention of a neighbor woman. She poked her head in to see what was going on. She understood enough English and with some hand signals explained that she knew people who could use some of the furniture and appliances we were going to throw away. She became my furniture distributor. A nice dining table, but way too big for Steve's place, found a new home. A wall unit became one less thing to truck away. She brought in neighbors, they salvaged what they wanted, and the rest we discarded.

We worked from seven in the morning until after seven at night. Marilyn was concerned about the excessive noise our demolition made in the early mornings and late evenings. We didn't want Steve getting into trouble with his neighbors, so Marilyn made up some nice little boxes of chocolates and got some flowers and gave them to the neighbors to smooth things over.

I would wake up at 3:00 am thinking about the things we had to get done that day. That's the way I work on a project. I was pushing Ken and the team pretty hard. Ken does great renovations on his own home but those were more of a hobby and could take up to six months. But the intensity of getting the project done in one week and coordinating so many people was a different level.

I was the foreman, naturally, which gave me time to make some calls to furniture and appliance companies. I knew the key people in those stores, told them Steve's story, and explained that soliciting was new for me. "I'm OK if you say no, because I say no often as well." I was totally surprised. All of them came through.

We put in new flooring, new furniture, new electronics, new appliances, and painted the walls. I put all new shelving in the closets. That's my specialty.

Steve uses a computer for work so we replaced his antiquated one with a new, faster computer and software that would allow him to stream to a new 65" TV screen. Steve Saint, Creekside's IT tech, came over to ensure everything was hooked up well.

Brian and Leti, owners of Cabinet Effects, a kitchen cabinet company, donated and installed a complete new kitchen as well as bathroom shelves. We got Steve power blinds for the windows and a power desk that could be adjusted. It really worked well with his wheelchair.

The before and after pictures told the story. On the Saturday, we invited the team and anyone else who wanted to be part of it to come to the unveiling and celebrate with Steve. His sister, Judy, and his brother-in-law were tearful from joy on the reveal day. Judy was amazing at helping remove and re-position Steve's personal effects while sorting what went back into the apartment. I'm not sure what the manager was expecting from a group of volunteers when he came in for a look. "Wow, this is really nice. This would have taken us a month to do." He was pleasantly surprised with the finished product.

I love those projects, although I must admit, Ken and I went at it hard. We were a bit tired. I might be over 70, but the brain is working fine.

Find a way or make a way.

Our condo is on the top floor of a 23-floor development: 3,500 square feet, towering ceilings, lots of natural light and a spacious floor plan. Marilyn had free rein to furnish it. That was a trade-off for her not wanting to move out of our former condo. "I just made this place the way I like it. I thought we would be here for a long time."

Marilyn went to work with her longtime friend, Silvana Lewis. She is amazing. We first met her when we were putting together our daughter's wedding in 1995. From there she helped us decorate our homes and became Marilyn's dear friend. She's got the wow factor. Marilyn always has Silvana by her side when she's shopping and designing. We love everything she does. The three of us went to the High Point Furniture Market in North Carolina, the largest dealer-only furniture show in the world. There are presentations, keynote speakers, and showrooms featuring the best and latest designs. Furniture dealers come from across North America and around the world. This was the place to be to see how environments could be created for beautiful homes.

While I worked in the Magnussen showroom, Marilyn and Silvana shopped the furniture market. Then they gave me a tour to see if I liked their choices.

My first reaction was, "Ladies, you have no idea what you're creating here. We have a problem." I pointed out that they had chosen furniture proportionate to the size of the rooms, which was smart, but there was no way of getting furniture that size to the 23rd floor. The pieces were so large that they weren't going to fit in the elevator. A building of this magnitude should have a freight elevator, but it didn't. Silvana, who's quick witted, says, "You're operations. You can figure it out, no problem."

When I explained the situation to the owner of our building he said, "Let's talk to my guy that's supervising the construction of the condo."

We explored all kinds of ideas.

Put it on the top of the elevator. That's risky and it's not even safe. And who knows what the furniture would look like when it gets up to the 23rd floor. Scrap that idea.

Ask movers to carry the fourteen pieces up the stairs. Twenty-three flights? They said, "We don't think so." And I didn't blame them.

"The only other way is to hoist them up by crane. I can hook you up with the crane guy who worked on this building. But he'll have to rent a crane, get a permit, shut down the street, and reroute traffic. That will probably cost around $10,000."

Go big.

At 7:00 am the tractor trailers arrived on a perfect weather day—no wind, the air was still, and the cloudless sky promised the absence of rain all day long. The crane was the width of the street. They set up outriggers so that the crane wouldn't tip. They used booms to get the pieces higher than the 23rd floor so they could be swung onto the balcony. They had a guy directing the crane from the 23rd floor and men on the balcony to carry in the boxes. It was slick.

Marilyn got sandwiches for the whole crew. We had a party. Spectators lined the street. Passersby shaded their eyes against the sun to gaze up twenty-three stories to catch a glimpse of what was going on. It was a big deal. Marilyn told her small group about the action and the girls said, "We're coming over." Our daughter Laura showed up. They sipped tea and coffee on the sidewalk patio of a little cafe across the street from our building. A ringside view of the operation and the spectators. Laura heard more than one passerby say, "What are they doing? Why wouldn't they just use the elevator?"

The workers finished unboxing the furniture, piled the cardboard on the balcony, lifted the sling and took it all down in one trip. The work was done, everything was cleaned up and the crane was on its way by three o'clock, ahead of schedule.

And that's the way Magnussens get stuff done.

The day made an impression on the residents of our building. We would be in the elevator for weeks after that day, introducing ourselves because everyone was new to the building. We'd ask each other, "When did you move in? What's your name? What floor do you live on?" And the light bulb would go on.

"Oh, you're on the top floor. You're the ones that brought your furniture in by crane!"

And we'd say, "Yes. That's us."

And people would ask every time, "Why didn't you put the furniture on the elevator?"

"It didn't fit."

While they didn't say it out loud, you could hear the wheels turning, "What kind of furniture do they have?"

We wouldn't let a little problem like large furniture with no freight elevator stop us. I'm the operations guy, right? We found a way.

Go big.

When I hit 50, I started a new chapter of my life.

I went for a physical. My doc said, "Your bad cholesterol is good, and your good cholesterol is bad. You need to work out in the gym, do some weight resistance but do it in moderation." He knows me.

I went to the gym.

Got in shape.

Lost 40lbs.

I learned how to run on a treadmill. Intervals are the key. You walk with no incline. Then you set it on incline and run for two minutes to get your heart rate up. Then you bring it down. That flushes blood through your system and cleans up anything along the sides of the arteries. I discovered that a treadmill is better for training because you can adjust it for intervals. Outdoors you don't naturally have hills every two minutes.

In Florida there is a gym close to our home. We walk or ride our bikes to it. I have a nice gym in the building in Waterloo where we live, and we have one in our cottage too.

The exercise was good, but I probably overdid it.

That may have been what triggered my A-fib.

I'm so competitive. I can push myself too hard with a trainer. He says, "Do this," and I want to do more. I'm like a kid. It's something in me that is hard to describe. I am inclined to take everything to extremes.

If you say I can have a candy, I'll say, "What's wrong with eating the whole package?"

When I do something, it's full-bore. Go big.

I've got to watch that I don't overdo it. By overdoing it I mean I'm still probably above average for my age in a lot of categories, but my mind thinks I am 35. I have to remember that my systems are a little bit used.

I see a specialist in Toronto, Doctor Chen. He's fantastic. He heads up the St. Michael's hospital. Dr. Chen is from Hong Kong. He spends about fifty per cent of his time there. We talk about Hong Kong and doing business in China. He's a bit of an entrepreneur in his profession and he's got his own clinic with numerous surgeons working for him.

One time, Marilyn and I arrived at 11:00 in the morning for my regular check-up. The process was rigorous. We weren't done until 4:30. There were tests and ultrasounds. They had me run on a treadmill. When you get off the treadmill, your heart rate should go down. Well, mine shot up, scared the nurse technician. She called a doctor and they put me on a monitor.

When they caught my heart rate on the monitor it was 225. That's dangerous. That's stroke area. Or heart failure. About one in five people in North America over the age of 40 will develop heart failure. And the average life expectancy following heart failure is measured at around 2.1 years, at a tremendous impact to quality of life

He diagnosed me with A-fib.

Atrial fibrillation is often called A-fib. It is the most common type of treated heart arrhythmia. An arrhythmia is when the heart beats too slowly, too fast, or in an irregular way.

I was a candidate to have ablation surgery.

With ablation they go in and basically cauterize where they think the pulses are telling the brain to speed up when they shouldn't. I don't know the ins and outs, but it's pretty interesting technology.

The doctor said, "I can get you in hopefully in a year, but it could be 17 months for that surgery because everything is so backed up."

Wow.

Not too long after, I happened to be talking with my lawyer and mentioned the wait for ablation surgery. He said, "You need to go to Cleveland Clinic." I said, "Tell me about Cleveland Clinic." He had his aorta replaced there. He says, "You need to go to Cleveland."

I talked to Dr Chen about Cleveland because I was afraid that he was going to get bent out of shape because I was going to the US. And he said, "If you can afford it, I recommend it. That's where I was trained and that's where all my surgeons go to get trained. It's the best hospital in the world." He sold me on it.

My lawyer gave me the person to contact and three weeks later Marilyn and I were on our way for the operation with Dr. Tarakji. He is a world-class physician and thought leader in the advanced treatment of atrial fibrillation, and a great guy personality-wise. He received his medical degree from Damascus University Faculty of Medicine and has been in practice for more than 20 years. I asked him how many surgeries he has performed. He didn't know, but at least several thousand.

The hospital facility in Cleveland is amazing. The patient pays for it, but the care is incredible. The operational designers paid attention to detail. Big, wide halls. In the hospital lobby there was a cello and a grand piano being played. Beautiful music, very relaxing. It's helpful. Most people get nervous about going in.

When I went into surgery, every person that was going to work on me shook my hand and said, "This is what I'm going to do in the process." There were a lot of people who were going to be in the operating room. I loved the 72-inch TV that my toes were touching, which is how they monitored the process. They go in through the groin and up to your heart on both sides. Then they do their thing for five hours.

The technical explanation for the procedure is a little more precise. A surgeon inserts catheters into a blood vessel in the groin and threads them up to the heart, giving access to the inside of the heart. The doctor then uses the catheters to scar a small area of the heart by making small burns or small freezes. In the burning process, a type of energy called radiofrequency energy uses heat to scar the tissue. The freezing process involves a technique called cryoablation. Scarring helps prevent the heart from conducting the abnormal electrical signals that cause atrial fibrillation.

Post-op, Dr. Tarakji said, "In a few days you'll be back in the gym." And on day three, I wasn't sure he was correct. But sure enough, I felt great in six days. The incision is the part that bothers you the most, but it's not that bad. Ablation is a miracle of surgery. Unbelievable. I did have one of the best surgeons in the world do it because Cleveland is the number one heart hospital in the world.

Marilyn stayed at the hospital hotel. She just walked across the corridor to get back to her room. It's a beautiful hospital. She was a rock. When we had our last check up, Dr. Tarakji said, "Here's a bunch of restaurants. I recommend you take Marilyn somewhere she would like."

When I was at the Cleveland Clinic, they were trying to figure out how I got A-fib. "Do you have sleep insomnia?" I said, no. Marilyn said, "Yes. He stops breathing when he's sleeping sometimes."

The other thing he asked was, "Were you ever a marathon or triathlon runner?" I said, "Well, thanks for asking, but no." Those two activities seem to be where they believe a lot of A-fib comes from, because your heart's getting shocked regularly.

I go back to Dr Chen every year and he says, "You don't need to come back to me." I said, "Well, I just like coming to see a doctor."

Dr Chen is a big believer in Apple Watch. He's written articles on it. Twenty-five smart watches were tested for efficiency and Apple came out on top. He explained that I can do my own ECG on my Apple watch. I send my readings over the year to him before I go in to see him. At our last appointment he said, "I use you as an example when I lecture. I don't use your name, but I tell my students that you send me all the data on your heart from over the year." He said, "That's good because that watch on your wrist is what my $70,000 monitor does."

Tracking data with my watch gives him a view of my heart over time. The benefit is a patient's heart rate might be high just because they're coming to see the doctor. They're anxious about the results. Tracking over time with a smart watch takes away that factor. He says we're always trying to manage information. He sees the future of medicine with monitors on our wrist, rather than just doing what they've always done.

I'm grateful that these specialists provided me with being able to enjoy many more Christmases with my family.

Marilyn loves everything Christmas.

We have two storage cages for our condo in Waterloo. One is basically for Christmas decorations. On November 1st, my loving wife insists that we put up a Christmas tree and decorations even though we will leave in mid-December to celebrate Christmas in Florida. The first year of this exercise, I tried to reason with her not to bother as we would only see the tree for a few weeks. That wasn't my finest negotiation. Every year since then, if I protest, she gets pretty wound up, so I say, "OK, I know honey, don't worry, it's going to be done." I dutifully haul the tree and the boxes of decorations out of the storage cage, bring them up twenty-three flights on the elevator, cart them into the living room and set up the tree. It usually takes a few weeks to decorate the entire condo.

Christmas is a generous time for hospitality. That's a big deal. Most days during the festive season, our condo is filled with friends and family. One year there were fourteen family members who stayed for seventeen days with us in Florida. We loved it! Most of them were able to work online which was great.

Marilyn is super organized and loves to cook and lay out a nice spread, but holidays afford time for her to take a night off and go with the family to a restaurant. It's quite an entourage when all fourteen of us arrive. She makes all the restaurant reservations months in advance. She learned that the hard way. One year she called over a month in advance and all the restaurants were booked. She was informed she'd need to call in early fall.

Dinners at home usually conclude with coffee, tea, dessert, and a reading from the Bible followed by lots of discussion. It's an interesting dynamic now that the grandkids are older. One evening we choose a charitable project for the coming year, and there is usually a good back and forth before we decide. Usually, we end up with more than one.

On Christmas Day we read the story of the nativity from the Bible as one way to keep the meaning of the day in front of us. Opening gifts with the whole family takes at least three hours. But it's more than just opening gifts. Everybody opens their gift and everyone else focuses on that person.

Every Christmas is a reminder that God spared my life from heart problems and allowed me to go big in helping people like Steve. Every day is a gift and I never take even one of them for granted.

Chapter 15, Go Big

Find a way or make a way is what going big is all about. If you commit and stay the course, and if you recommit and recommit again when it seems improbable or even impossible, you will probably win. There's not much outside that can stop you when nothing restricts your forward motion on the inside. Be kind. Be caring. Be patient. Be forgiving. Be positive. Be present. Walk in the other person's shoes.

- Are you ready to do whatever it takes to accomplish something essential for your family or others?
- Think about one area of life where you need to "find a way or make a way." What action you will take to do that?

CHAPTER

16

GENEROSITY

OUR ELDEST DAUGHTER, LISA, CAME TO ME WITH AN intriguing question when she was around fourteen years old. "Dad, are you a millionaire?"

She caught me off guard. "What would make you ask?"

"Oh, one of my friends said, 'You have a lot of things, and a beautiful house. Your dad must be a millionaire.' I told her I didn't know. Are you?"

I simply responded, "We have assets that equal a million." The answer was enough to send her on her carefree way.

That brief exchange made me feel good. Lisa had never even thought about our family in those terms because we didn't put people in classes of nice homes and not-nice homes. It was no big deal to her. Marilyn and I purposed to raise our kids without entitlement. Kelly arrived when we lived in a modest, one-bedroom apartment. Our kids didn't think of our family as "rich." It's a credit to parents when some kids grow up and don't know they were poor, and some kids grow up and don't think they were rich. Magnussen kids never wanted for anything, but they worked for everything. Not that we weren't generous in providing for them, but we wanted them to learn the discipline of being responsible for making their own way in life.

Words matter. I am happy and humbled by the words that my kids have expressed about their dad.

I highly respect him.

I love him more than he knows.

I feel very honored to call him Dad.

I consider it a true joy and blessing that the Lord gave me him as my dad.

I'm very proud of him.

I think he's very wise.

He's humble.

He's quick to give credit to everybody else and not to himself.

He's intentional.

He's quiet about his generosity.

I struggle with generosity. Not the giving but the anonymity. I wonder if I should have been more open with my kids. I share the last quality in that list with my dad. He would never talk about his generosity. He quietly gave so that no one other than Mom, Alice, me, and the beneficiaries were aware. And most times even the beneficiaries did not know the source of their support.

I have a friend who loves being generous. There were some important homeless, addiction and recovery projects in our city that needed funding. They wanted to get some beds to help kids on drugs. He said, "We need to give $350,000 each." And there was a bunch of us that did. But then the organization wanted to put our names on the building to say thanks. And I said, "You can just leave my name off."

It's the same with all the grandkids. They know how generous we are with them, but we're very quiet about what we do for other people. We're not flashy and don't want credit. We have quietly given generously where there is a need; money, time, advice, or all three. Show me your bank account and calendar and I can see where your priority is. It is through serving God that teaches us many lessons in leadership. You'll be amazed at what insight you learn from service to others that helps in everyday life such as how to manage people or how to deal with your attitude. I learned that you cannot outgive God.

In Creekside's early days, volunteers were responsible for all the programs. One of my oversights was LifeGroups, which were mid-week gatherings in the homes of congregants. As more and more people became part of the church, the responsibility became increasingly difficult to manage in a volunteer role. I said to our pastor, "If we want this ministry to flourish, we need to hire someone to lead the leaders of the groups."

"We don't have the funds."

"OK. Count on money for a salary for two years and hire someone."

Generosity is one of the requisite drivers for us because that's what keeps us grateful, and gratitude is the root of success.

We were committed to sharing the company's prosperity with those less fortunate by working with charities to alleviate poverty in the developing world through improving living conditions. We championed human rights, social awareness, and provided our international employees with education and training to create greater opportunities. Marilyn and I like to give to projects that have sustainable outcomes. There were projects in Haiti to support local businesses that would in turn help support the community. The idea there was to take the seawater and trench around it and as the water evaporates, they salvage all the salt. We resourced funds to build an elementary school in Uganda and provided the main meal for over 300 Muslim students every day. Many summer teams of teens have gone to Uganda from Creekside Church to have a firsthand cross-cultural encounter and serve as volunteers. The teens came home with an unforgettable life experience that shaped their worldview. I saw that effect firsthand from international business trips with our kids and in bringing our grandkids to Africa.

The year 2020 was our fiftieth wedding anniversary. Marilyn wanted to celebrate by inviting family and friends to dinner in the Walper Hotel Crystal Ball room where we had our original wedding reception. The COVID pandemic hit, and the world went on pause. We would have to wait. Months turned into two years, but that gave us time to dream up a wild idea. What if we celebrated by taking our family to Africa on a ten-day safari led by our friend Ryan?

Dr. Ryan Snider is a professor at the University of Waterloo in the discipline of cultural geography. He wrote his Ph.D. thesis on Land Tenure, Ecotourism and Sustainable Livelihoods, so it's no surprise he is the founding owner of the Socially Responsible Safaris company. Ryan was a classmate of our kids in junior high and remains friends with Laura to this day. He ate enough food in our home that we thought of him as family. We worked together on the facility development committee of Creekside. Ryan's one of the young entrepreneurs I get to mentor and share some of the things I've learned the hard way.

When COVID hit and shut down the safari business, Ryan's drivers struggled to feed their families. They emailed often asking if he had any work for them, so Ryan and his wife, Liza, brainstormed ideas to help them survive. Because Kenya is famous for amazing coffee, they decided to start an import coffee business and the safari drivers were used to bring the coffee beans from the farms to transports, weigh the beans, and properly load the trucks. I shared what I had learned about US customs and container insurance. Coffee became a stopgap until the pandemic ended. The safari business took off because everybody wanted to travel again, and their coffee business is doing very well.

Ryan's safari company promises adventurers a discovery-filled journey off the beaten path. Marilyn always wanted to go on a safari, me not so much, but we went together to Kenya in 2014 and I'm not sure who loved the experience more. We traveled with our friends, Steve and Sue Scherer, to Nairobi and then to Lake Naivasha. Ryan took us on a boat to see hippos drinking by the shore and we were so close we could almost touch them. Then we went to the famous Masai Mara and back to Nairobi.

Ryan and his wife Liza guide their safaris with one goal: to provide an opportunity to learn about the world, thereby inspiring people to create positive change. Each year they organize several safaris designed to encourage intercultural learning and create economic and environmental benefits for schools, health clinics, and orphanages along their safari routes. I respect their organization's commitment to social responsibility: people, planet, and profit. Their clients use locally owned hotels, vehicles, and river boats, so the money goes into the local economy, not an American-owned corporation. The Sniders' organization takes only a three percent administration fee because they volunteer their time, so clients know their funds go directly to helping kids.

In the summer of 2022, fourteen Magnussens departed from Toronto, Raleigh, and Greensboro, and met up in Johannesburg, South Africa for the trip of our lifetimes. Ryan took us to Chobe Game Park and Okavango Delta, in Botswana, and Sabi Sands, South Africa. Chobe is famous because it's hot, and during the day, all wildlife comes down to the river. We were on a boat in the shade and the elephants came right to the boat, grazing by water.

Ryan organized projects for us like he does for all his guests. He took us to a local market and sent the grandkids on a scavenger hunt. He pointed to each of them, "You go and get beans, and you get rice, and you get cooking oil, and you get toilet paper." The kids had a blast. Then we loaded the vehicles, drove a couple kilometers to an orphanage, and delivered the supplies. A director at the institution welcomed us and explained who they were and what they were accomplishing in the lives of children. The rest of the day our family delivered supplies, played games with the children, and got to hold babies. The grandkids got to observe people's reaction and felt the joy of giving. At the end of each day, we enjoyed dinners of local dishes under the stars on warm African evenings, talking about what happened that day. Ryan did an incredible job of drawing the kids out with questions.

The only hiccup on the entire trip was when one of the single prop Cessnas used to shuttle us around broke down the morning we were going to the last game park. Ryan and I looked at each other, saying, "Oh boy, how will they get a part to replace the plane in this remote area?" They solved the problem better than we ever dreamed. There are a lot of mining executives in the region with private jets and helicopters to get into remote locations. We never missed a beat.

The safari company arranged for a private Leer jet, picked up some of our group, flew to a bigger airport, and then brought them to Sabi Sands by helicopter. The rest of the family had left earlier on a second plane with no idea of the extraordinary adventure that was unfolding. The first group arrived before us and hid, so when we arrived, they jumped out to surprise us. "How did you get here so fast?" We told the story and then everybody was wishing they could have been on the jet, because we'd had an incredible experience. The kids had never been on a helicopter before, let alone a Leer jet.

Following the trip, Marilyn and Hayley put together a photo album filled with memories and comments. Paisley and Brody summed up the sentiments of the whole family. "The best part of this trip was meeting all the wonderful, sweet people and all of the animals that God created" (Paisley). "My favorite part of this trip was seeing all the amazing animals and spending time with family. This is a trip I will never forget" (Brody).

We are grateful for treasured memories of travel adventures, boat excursions, and tranquil vacation days at the cottage.

Summer Sunday mornings at the cottage means we pack everyone up and caravan into Sauble Beach for church. We've done that for years. One Sunday morning, the last amen was prayed, the auditorium had emptied, and Kelly, along with some hungry grandkids, stood in the parking lot, impatiently waiting for the ladies to stop talking. Kelly doesn't remember why the subject came up, but he asked his nephew, Brody, if he knew that Papa had donated money to purchase the lots that this church is on. Brody's look of surprise said it all.

I inherited fifteen commercial lots in Sauble Beach from my father. He was a keen investor. You can never own enough land, especially in a growing community with a popular beach. The brother-in-law of a friend of mine was a pastor of Sauble Christian Fellowship. Tim had planted the church years ago in an unused fire hall and as the church grew, he moved it to the Community Centre. I meet with the pastors for coffee because sometimes pastors need someone to talk with. The wife of one of the pastors told me how much her husband loved our meetings.

They needed land to build a facility that would help fulfill their vision of being a beacon of hope on Lake Huron. We donated money to help the church purchase lots adjacent to ones we owned. The congregation kept growing so the plan was to add on an expansion, but they were short of land for a required septic system and parking lot. Donating seven of our lots helped them out, two for the septic and five for parking.

A feature of the church was a large lighthouse that people could see from the highway. During the expansion they were thinking of choosing to save costs in the six-figure range by reducing the height of a new lighthouse. But doing so would not make it visible to traffic. I said, "Over the long term it'll be a good marker for people to see and wonder what's that all about," so they built it to the requisite height.

I learned to be cautious about becoming the donor of a big percentage of a church's operating budget because that can become a real problem. As much as it's wonderful to give, relying on a single donor for operations can get a church built up beyond what the people can sustain and then there's pressure. In the early days of Creekside, I saw the liability when a significant part of the operational budget was carried by one giver, and I was convicted that it wasn't wise stewardship for the church. When one person or family is relied on to that degree others don't see the need to step in. All it takes in that instance is for a business to go into crisis to put a church in jeopardy. Capital projects are different because they are a one-time initiative to get a church to the next level.

Stewardship is "the careful and responsible management of something entrusted to one's care" (Merriam-Webster).

Of the forty parables that Jesus told, more than twenty-five percent of them had to do with money. He taught more about money than on faith and prayer combined. There are more than 2300 verses in the Bible on money, wealth, and possessions.

A stingy planter gets a stingy crop; a lavish planter gets a lavish crop. I want each of you to take plenty of time to think it over and make up your own mind what you will give. That will protect you against sob stories and arm-twisting. God loves it when the giver delights in the giving."
— 2 Corinthians 9:6-7 (MSG)

I started my career with $38,000 in sales. I figured our manufacturing would be a local Canadian business for my entire career. That would have been great, but my partner had a bigger idea. I had no idea that by the time I retired we would be producing 150,000 pieces of furniture a month, selling furniture to over twenty countries, working with governments, and having 10,000 people make our furniture. What I find humorous is being elected chairman of American Home Furnishing. In human terms I should have had an MBA or a degree in economics, or degrees in managing cultures and people. What I had was a partner named Jesus.

There were many corrective lessons I learned, but I feel blessed and full of joy to be able to steward what God has given me.

When I was a young adult, one of my mentors tried to educate me about the hidden failures of success. I say tried because his wisdom was sage advice, but my mind couldn't fully appreciate the value of his warning. Arden Mertz was a college professor and a leader at our church. He warned, "Richard, the number one risk is success." I was too far away from success for his words to sink in, but I've since seen that to be the experience of so many, including me.

Honda was the number one car company in the world at one time. Their president said that success was his biggest concern. There's nothing wrong with success, but it has incredible potential to become dangerous for your team, for your company, and for yourself. Pride is subtle. Arrogance can sneak up on you, and before you know it you're looking at a free fall like Magnussen experienced in 2008.

Pride goes before destruction, a haughty spirit before a fall.
— Proverbs 16:18 (NIV)

When a company starts to soar there's always a risk that you start thinking better of yourself than you should. You stop paying attention to the little things that made you a success in the first place. Your customers are thrilled with you. Everybody is calling your name. In 2006 when Magnussen was flying high, I stepped back from the daily operations to become involved in charitable and philanthropic endeavors. Two years later, an economic crisis caught me off guard with how quickly the company went off the rails. The truth is the fall wasn't fast. It happened slowly over months, one ill-advised decision after another, until it left us exposed to a downturn.

I had let go of my obsessive attention to detail because I had become impressed with our success and the accolades we were getting. Jim Collins didn't write his book, *How the Mighty Fall*, until four years later. Too bad. I could have used his wisdom about what he calls "the hubris born of success." Collins says, "Accumulated momentum can carry an enterprise forward, for a while, even if its leaders make poor decisions or lose discipline."

I thought back to the president of Honda. He was wise. When you become number one, an arrogance can go through your company like a virus. "We are the best." Even if it's not said, it's implied. Maybe you're short with a customer. Maybe you stop making calls to customers who aren't the biggest customers. Maybe you leverage your company into a danger zone, and no one notices because the bright lights of hubris are in your eyes. It happens to all of us. Is it happening to you?

However, there is good news. It's through those tough times and adversity that a person or a company can become stronger. That was our experience in 2010. We had an incredible bounce back. Whether you attribute it to God or some other factor, humility is the only way back from a fall. For me, it was "humble yourself in the sight of God and he will lift you up." We faced reality, re-employed rigorous measures, tightened our belts, trimmed our staff, determined to lower our debt load, and did a lot of praying and handholding. And God blessed Magnussen with a better position than we had experienced. Life lessons can have short shelf lives. It's important if once burned to be twice shy.

By 2010, Magnussen Home Furnishings employed 160 workers in offices and manufacturing centers around the world. In the middle of a recession,

Magnussen sales grew 13.5 per cent in the second quarter of 2009. Our brand continued to grow and evolve, adjusting to changing customer trends and market demands while being grounded on trust, honesty, and respect.

We had a renewed focus on developing relationships, infrastructure, and skills between 2000 and 2010, which empowered us to provide our customers with beautifully designed, high quality, high value furnishings, delivered in lead times and at service levels that were unrivalled in the industry. In 2002, Magnussen-Presidential Furniture became Magnussen Home. The addition of "Home" reflects who we are and what we offer as a company: fine furniture, designed for today's lifestyles, created by a family of craftsmen from around the world to enhance the most important rooms in your home.

On occasion, my beliefs have led me to run counter to conventional business wisdom. The Toronto international annual furniture showcase, through the Ontario Furniture Manufacturers' Association (OFMA), was literally the high point of the Canadian industry year. We depended on the show for a good portion of our sales. It was like Black Friday, only exclusively for furniture. Salespeople relied on it for a significant portion of their commissions. One year I sensed that God was saying, "Close your wholesale showroom on Sundays." What? The impression was clear and persistent. This was going to be another one of those times when it felt like God was asking us to give away all of our savings.

Everybody thought I was absolutely crazy. The salespeople particularly said, "That's our biggest day. How can we do this?" I had a lot of very concerned salespeople. But we put a sign out that read, "Closed for Family Day." I didn't know what would happen, but I felt this would be good for everyone, including the salespeople, in the long run.

And what do you know? We ended up having increased sales. How did that happen? As somebody told me, "Anybody that would have the courage to do that can be trusted." Sales rose by over twenty-five per cent that year. Go figure. I certainly didn't make the choice out of a legalistic religious value. The practice wasn't followed for very long. I didn't feel the need to. It was one more time that God reminded me that humble trust was as much a part of the bottom line as marketing and sales.

The Canadian Home Furnishings Alliance (CHFA) established the Lifetime Achievement Award to recognize those individuals who over their lifetime have made exemplary and sustained contributions to the Canadian home furnishings industry and their communities. The CHFA concluded that such an award was appropriate for me. I was 59, an age that seemed short for a lifetime.

Susan Down from the *Toronto Star* made the trek to Kitchener for a sit-down interview. She was good at turning a phrase. "His business acumen is as strong and polished as the tables his father designed." She noted that "family involvement is the future as well as the past for the company. Richard's son Kelly is vice-president of sales and his son-in-law, Nathan Cressman, is vice-president of marketing and product development."

Concerns about Magnussen moving manufacturing out of North America were top of mind in the industry. When she addressed the subject, it was easy to justify our choice. "When we went international, we actually employed more Canadians locally than we did manufacturing. China is really ripe for Canadian-branded products. They are very much brand oriented, and they want to buy from the company that makes it. They could buy anything as a knock-off but there's a developing market that wants authentic brands."

Believe it or not, a star went along with the Alliance's presentation. Not a star in a hall of fame, a real star in outer space. The award came with a framed certificate and a map showing the celestial co-ordinates of a star named Richard Magnussen. I love the creative thinking and smart marketing behind the concept. If you focus a high-powered telescope on a clear night towards the Ursa Major RA 11h 14m 28s D 59' 29' you might see my star when you look up.

Though you can't see them all in one glance, there's a billion trillion stars in the known universe.

There's not much I enjoy more than on a clear night, sitting on the patio at our cottage or on the pool deck in Florida, and gazing up into a starry sky. There's something about that view that puts any challenges in front of me into perspective. Rather than feeling insignificant because I am one of eight billion people on a planet that is one of a billion trillion planets in a universe that is ever expanding, I am in awe of a Creator who is on record as numbering the ever-lessening hairs on my head. I'm aware that Jesus was using exaggeration to make a point when he said, "The very hairs of your head are numbered" (Matthew 10:30, NIV)

That understanding of God grows humility, not ego. Becoming humble isn't something that we can produce in ourselves. It is something that God must help us with and open our eyes to.

We use Lee Strobel's material at Creekside. Strobel was an atheist when he worked as an award-winning journalist for the Chicago Tribune. Strobel's wife became a believer in Jesus. He tried to prove her faith was all wrong, but he came to a different understanding of God after investigation of the evidence. He concluded that science points powerfully and persuasively toward the existence of a Creator who just happens to look a lot like the God of the Bible.

Strobel believes that science affirms Psalm 102:25, "In the beginning, God laid the foundations of the earth, and the heavens are the work of your hands."

The purpose of your life is far greater than your own personal fulfillment, your peace of mind or even your happiness. It's far greater than your family, your career or even your wildest dreams and ambitions. If you want to know why you were placed on this planet, you must begin with God. You were born by his purpose and for his purpose.

Humility precedes honor.
— Proverbs 15:33 (NLT)

Chapter 16, Generosity

Generosity is contagious: even a small gift activates a desire to respond in a similar way. One kindness can inspire other acts of kindness. And generosity impacts our health and well-being. It boosts mood, self-esteem, and reduces stress, anxiety, and blood pressure. Generous people are happy people. Generosity and humility work together in a counter-intuitive way. The humility required to let others know of your generosity is a nudge that can make a positive difference in their generosity. Giving is a virtuous circle.

- Are those closest to you aware of your choices related to giving?
- Could your story be the nudge that makes a difference?
- In what way could you be generous with your time, skills, or finances?

CHAPTER

17

RETIREMENT

LAURA, OUR LAST CHILD, WENT OFF TO TRINITY WESTERN University, so we felt like empty nesters. Our 5,000 square foot home began to feel mammoth. We discussed our next move.

Marilyn wanted to downsize, move back to Waterloo and be closer to her friends, the kids, and our church. So, she went looking and found a little, 1300 square foot condo. Talk about downsizing. We moved from 5000 square feet to 1300. It was a little romantic thing.

Then the grandkids started coming. When Lisa and Nathan came to Canada with Ty as a baby it was tight. Ty slept in the furnace room next to the treadmill in a play pen. We reversed course again and went back to 4000 square feet in a Deer Ridge subdivision for a few years.

Then we sold that in 2012 and purchased a condo that was under construction. Laura and Josh had just moved into a new home. We said to them, "If we help finish off your basement for you, could we live down there till our condo is ready?" We did have a fallback plan to go up to the cottage and live there if that didn't work. But we ended up living in Josh and Laura's basement. Most parents fear having adult kids living in their basement. Our kids had their parents living in their basement. But we got along so well. It was a win-win.

But who knew that would last for over two years?

Laura is super organized. When the basement was being finished for our living area, she supervised all the construction. She got along well with the contractors, got things done, and Marilyn had her new nest. The by-product was that they had live-in nannies.

Paisley, their youngest, was born in 2013. Brody was six, and Lola was two. That made three preschoolers and four adults under one roof. It was so fun. Laura and Marilyn organized the duties. I was the clean-up guy. When the babies needed an arm, they handed them off to me. Marilyn trucked Brody around, doing laundry and making meals.

By the time our condo was ready, Marilyn had become pretty attached to the living arrangements and our grandkids. "I don't know if I really want to move."

I told her, "That's OK, honey. I'm leaving on this date and moving in, and you come when you feel like you want to."

Marilyn said to Josh, "You'll be so glad to get rid of your in-laws after us being here for two and a half years."

"No, actually. I'm going to really miss you guys."

When we moved out, Paisley couldn't understand. Grandparents in the basement was all she knew.

In 2016, I became the first Canadian to be elected chairman of the board of the American Home Furnishings Alliance (AHFA). Based in High Point, North Carolina, the AHFA represents over 2,000 leading furniture manufacturers and distributors and over 2000 suppliers to the furniture industry worldwide. I was named to the post during the organization's annual general meeting. The role started on January 1st and lasted for the year 2017.

I was pleased to accept the role because I felt I needed to give back to the industry that was very good to our company, much like I did with the Ontario Furniture Manufacturers Association when I served on their board and as president. Magnussen Home does about 80% of our business in the U.S., and it was important to stay in touch with this marketplace. The AHFA was very focused on regulations, which is critical to manage as an industry, and works very closely with the U.S. federal government on consumer safety issues.

I wanted to do whatever I could to help the industry work closer with retailers on the tip-over issue. That's when a piece of furniture can be easily tipped over by a toddler. Home accidents were bringing devastating heartache to young American families. A child was dying every two weeks, and thousands of people had been injured. I hoped my presence would influence the AHFA to work with Canadian industry associations and the Canadian government to ensure uniform regulations across North America. Canadian regulatory bodies benefited from the work the AHFA team had done in the U.S. on this issue and adopted the U.S. tip-over consumer guidelines.

As a brash young college student, I told my father I might be bored working at his company. After 46 years, I never found that boring day. I retired in 2016.

Retirement can be a taxing thing. Suddenly, a retired husband is around all the time. That can spell big trouble. It has for some friends of mine. I'd heard people explain retirement: "You wake up in the morning. There's nowhere you should be. No to-do lists. You read the paper, do whatever you want. That's great for the first week, or maybe month. But then after that, it's 'get me out of here!'"

I knew that it wouldn't go well for me to become Marilyn's sous chef. I do chop vegetables for her, and I've learned how to use the washing machine, but that kind of work is not challenging enough for me, having come out of an intense business life. Marilyn and I know how to give each other space. We were each used to being on our own because I traveled a lot for the business. So, it's not like being away from each other for a short time was a big deal. She goes to be with the kids in North Carolina a couple of times a year. I think she really likes that.

Buying a place in Florida was at the top of my retirement bucket list. Dad and Mom had a place there, and I learned to love the area. When I retired, Marilyn said she wanted to travel. And I said, "OK, we can travel." She said, "But let's just rent in Florida." I said, "OK, I'll buy, and you be my tenant." She just shook her head.

We bought our home in Naples, Florida, so the kids and grandkids would have a destination they would want to go to where we could be with them. Our granddaughters in university and college love to come and visit Nana and

Papa. They bring school friends with them and hang out. Marilyn's so good at cooking. She prepares delicious meals, desserts, and coffees that keep them at the table. I tease the girls about the prospects on campus, and they're happy to give me an education in cultural terminology.

Marilyn and I enjoy a night out together at a restaurant. Ocean Prime in Naples is her favorite. A steak dinner and potatoes. She loves different kinds of salads, especially ones with beets and goat cheese. And then a nice crème brûlée to enjoy a leisurely finish to the meal.

I've always been a pretty good dresser. We were business casual in the office, but since I retired, I'm not as fussy about how I look when I go out. Maybe that's a little harsh. And that sounds like I look terrible, but that's not accurate. I'll throw on whatever, and it's good enough. Marilyn has a higher standard. I've been sent back to change on more than one occasion. I understand that what I wear is a little bit of a reflection on her. I've heard her say, "Look at that guy. Seriously, his wife let him go out like that?"

Friends wondered what I would do with all my free time. Build grandfather clocks? I loved that stuff. Years ago, I made a grandfather clock for my mother and one for Marilyn. I did that for 47 years, from being able to make furniture to seeing it done in mass production on an international scale. But I have no desire to go back and build a piece of furniture. I'm not looking for woodworking to relax or to have fun. I would rather make a deal buying a place, fixing it, flipping it, and turning a profit. I love the intrigue of that. I want to stay busy. I never complained about going to work. I like working. I'm challenged by making things better and making a profit.

Projects, I like projects, almost as much as I like getting on the water with fast boats. Silvana, our interior designer who worked on the majority of our homes, was helpful to Marilyn. She suggested, "You know, Richard's been running a large, international business for so many years, and you think he's retiring. He needs an outlet." Marilyn just shook her head.

In 2015, we started in the direction of my dream of owning a home in Florida by renting a house. The next step was to find something more permanent. I have an eye for potential, so I'm always on the lookout for a house with an upside. For me, a realtor's sign on the front lawn of a house signals opportunity. I look for projects that have problems—ones that have gone cold on the real estate market, ones no one would touch. I look at a cold property and imagine, *OK, what are the issues?*

After watching me for fifty years, Marilyn says I have a gift. I can take something in which others see no value and envision what it could be. When we built our cottage, it was like that. Forty acres on Georgian Bay. Marilyn said, "How will you ever figure out how to do this?" I walked through the bush, got poison ivy a couple of times, and figured out where to put the cottage, the boathouse, and the landscaping. That's what I love. I always wanted to be an architect or a builder. Being in the furniture business, I saw how they all work together. If you buy right, you can redo things well and sell for a profit.

In 2015, a Florida real estate agent showed me a house that had no curb appeal, but the location and the structure of the house were good. We spent the next six months overseeing renovations from Canada on the exterior and interior. It's a relatively smaller house, but with the renovations, the neighbors say it's one of the cutest properties on our street.

We purchased that house and moved in April 2016.

Then I noticed a house nine doors down from ours. It was brand new and never lived in. It had been on the market for a relatively long time. For some reason, the whole real estate community had gone cold on this house. Properties in our neighborhood typically sold quickly. After watching the property for a few months, I called around to real estate agents to see what the issue was. Sure enough, there was a problem. Agents didn't want to sell the house because of its liabilities that would run them into issues with potential buyers. Buyers in our neighborhood want turnkey property. No muss, no fuss. This was not one of those types of properties.

I did a walkthrough with an engineer and a builder and asked them to see what could possibly be wrong. They quickly noted that there was a seawall from the 70s that had broken down. A new dock had been built over the seawall to cover the problem. However, one corner of the pool deck was beginning to fall into the canal. For some buyers, that looked like an enormous problem. I brought in an engineer and ran some cost estimates and calculated that we could turn a tidy profit with an expensive but workable fix. The property had a huge upside.

I told Marilyn I wanted to buy that house.

She said, "Oh, you don't want to buy that house."

I told her, "I can see an opportunity here."

I went in with confidence knowing I could fix the problems, so I made an offer 40% below the asking price. In real estate, you make your money on the buy. The owner accepted our offer. We bought the house and got to work.

The house didn't have a warm appeal outside or inside, but some fresh paint and new fixtures worked wonders. We tore out the old seawall and dock, installed a new seawall and dock, and repaired the deck. We rented our first home and moved into this new one.

Properties on our street rent for six figures a month. We live in Canada for six months of the year and six months in Florida. So, we quickly found renters for our new home, and the real estate agent who sold us our first house became our rental property manager.

We like to live free in Florida. The income from our properties more than covers our living expenses. Marilyn and I set up R&M Home Development for the construction of new homes and renovation of older homes. We purchased and flipped three houses in five years on the same street in Naples, Florida. I was getting quite a reputation. Neighbors wondered if I was going to buy the entire street, but that wasn't my intention. There are older homes on our street. They're nice homes, but they're purchased for the land value, torn down, and rebuilt. What was 2,500 square feet becomes 5,000 square feet. Florida is a fun place to do this.

Marilyn and I made an agreement. If I buy and renovate a property, we won't be moving into it. We'll sell it. She doesn't like moving locations. And even though the best way to make a profit from a tax standpoint is to live in it and then sell it, we have that understanding.

Flipping properties is what I would rather do than sit on a beach.

The cost of doing business increased by thirty to forty percent the longer we lived in Florida. Not everyone can compete in that market. Most home buyers would look at a house and see that it's somewhat unattractive inside, and they would walk away. That's how it is in Naples. They don't put mortgages on those houses; it's all cash.

The first house we purchased was valued at about half of what the second house cost us. The profit margin from the first wasn't enough to cover the difference, but we made the investment. I expected a market correction, but that didn't seem to be happening. Values kept going up. I asked a real estate agent in South Naples, "What's the deal? Things should be leveling off." He said, "Oh, they'll level off a little bit. But worldwide, there's about 10,000 people wanting to buy, and there are only 950 homes in South Naples. The demand is there." South Naples is known for its beautiful location, and even though the water levels are rising, we haven't had more hurricanes than a hundred years ago.

The third home is the one we currently live in. The fourth house we built on Marco Island, Florida. This was a project I went in on with a group of four businessmen from Kitchener-Waterloo. The house was finished in 2023 and sold while it was still under construction.

I love the process. The scorecard matters. The motivation is to make money on the play. People ask, "Why are you building another house? Why are you getting another condo?" Because I love the process. You can make good money on paper investments, but it's more fun when you can live in your investment.

Our youngest daughter, Laura, always likes to visit houses with me when she and her family come to visit. That is our thing. We will go to every open house. These are nice houses. People love to go around and see what's inside because they are usually furnished beautifully. The real estate guys have gotten to know me because it's not that big of an area.

In 2020, there was a brand-new house built on our street. I suggested that Laura and I should go look at it. Before we left, Marilyn said to Laura in jest, "Do not come home with a house, or you are going to be out of the will."

Laura and I had a walk-through. She said, "Wow, this is a nice house." When Laura came home, she said, "Mom, that's a nice house."

Marilyn said, "I know, I know. I don't want to look at it. I'm not going to go."

The funny part was Laura went back home on a Saturday, and Sunday afternoon Marilyn said, "I'd like to go across to that house and see it." I said, "You want to go and see that house?" And she said, "Yeah."

We work quickly. We weren't in the house for fifteen minutes. As we were crossing the street to go back home, Marilyn said, "I think we should put an offer on that house."

This is Marilyn.

I said, "OK, I think I need this in a recording."

We put in an offer that was accepted. Then COVID hit. I thought, "Oh man, I'm going to have two large houses on the same street. I don't really want that." But it turned out I had no problem renting our second house for a good price. So, the new one would carry itself.

We bought our present house because of the pool and the patio with an outdoor kitchen. We love it. It's beautiful.

But will it be the last one?

In addition to buying and flipping houses, Kelly and I bought shares in a company that owns RV and trailer storage places in Florida. The great thing about this investment is that I like working with my son. He's taking the lead. I'm not an RV specialist by any means. We have shares in one place in Sarasota and one in Punta Gorda. The company's owned by Canadians. We get a kick out of analyzing their operations, storage fees, and service fees. We think there's a lot of upside in cash flow and operations, but the bigger play on that investment is the real estate value. One of the places is on a four-lane highway in line for housing development. That's what we're keeping our eyes on.

After Hurricane Ian, the trailer storage business picked up. It was good before, but it's very good now because owners don't want to leave their boats close to the water in the offseason.

Despite all my projects, in our house the moments following dawn are usually a quiet time, especially after we became empty nesters. One of the first things I do is read something from the Bible. I wish I was 100% faithful every day, but it's my practice most days. When I was a teenager going to church, we called this having devotions. "You need to have your devotions every morning. Read your Bible and pray." That came across more like a duty than something enjoyable. I knew it was an important practice, but I didn't get into a daily habit until after Marilyn and I were married.

I'll read a few verses or maybe a whole chapter. Sometimes I'll follow a guide with a commentary on what the verses mean and how they can be applied to life. Starting my day that way gives me peace of mind. I probably didn't consciously realize it at the time, but adopting the habit of reading the Bible first thing in the morning was good for me. There were a lot of times when the business seemed especially challenging, or things were unsettled in our family. Words from the Bible gave me confidence that God was in control. It put my nerves and my thinking at peace. I was aware that I was hearing God's voice.

When our kids were young, we started mornings with reading verses from the book of Proverbs. We did that for years. When their kids were young, they followed that practice to some degree or other. The time of day isn't as important as reading the Bible at some time most days. To know that our grandkids have adopted that habit into their busy lives is fulfilling.

The YouVersion app is a great resource for reading the Bible on a smartphone. Over half a billion people have downloaded it. It's free. There are lots of translations of the Bible available as well as reading plans. I carried a Bible when I went to China and never knew if it was going to be confiscated. Being able to carry the Bible on an app was so helpful. Towards the end of my travel in China, the app was blocked, but there were ways to work around that through VPN.

Reading from the Bible regularly reminds me that God is present in my life. God is not far off. He is personal. My mother would say, "Richard, remember that Jesus is with you." Those words usually preceded me going on a date. But she wanted to remind me that God walks with me. That is true whether we acknowledge it or not. Starting the day being conscious of God's care for me is inspiring.

I enjoy a 45-minute walk most mornings. It's quiet, and I'm usually by myself. The air is fresh, and I try to keep the pace up. My heart gets a good workout, especially on the hills. I feel good when I walk. I have several favorite routes. One is called the Iron Trail. It goes through the city and on to the next community. It got its name because it is a paved-over railroad track. It's a popular walking trail used by a lot of people. I try to put in two and a half miles, sometimes three.

Waterloo Park is another trail. The path goes along a beachfront. It's lined with little umbrellas made from metal so they can go through the winter. When the sun shines, they sparkle. It's beautiful. There are a few hills in the park that add a bit of intensity to my walks.

I'm always thinking when I walk. I'll reflect on a passage from the Bible that I read that morning or heard on a Sunday at church. I'm mentoring some young business guys and I'll reflect on what we will talk about in our next meeting. If I'm going through a business transaction, I'll be trying to figure out what's the best scenario. I pray. I reflect on our kids.

One of the things I have observed was everybody wanting their kids to go to university and become a lawyer or an accountant. I've got nothing against a university education, but there are so many trades that get overlooked and can provide a fulfilling career.

I was always on the lookout for ways to advance our kids as they were growing up. Anything to give them a heads-up about a career path that might be right for them and a mindset that would make them employable. At Magnussen Homes, we set out to hire the best. Sometimes we used headhunters, but usually our HR department defined who we needed and would go searching for the right person. We looked for confident people, but that's a standard answer. Multiple interviews would give us insight into their self-awareness of weaknesses and strengths. We ran them through several assessment tools, including one called the Belbin Team Roles assessment. Most assessments focus on personality, but Belbin highlighted behavior, surfacing what represents a person best, what they know, and the way they think. Our company executives found the evaluations most helpful, so I was excited about having our kids discover how they might be best geared for a career.

When the kids got to grade eleven, they took the Myers-Briggs assessment. I liked that because they could discover something helpful about themselves. The kids liked it because their dad pulled them out of school. There was a company in London, Ontario, about an hour's drive away, where they could take the test. It took most of the day to answer the questions and then sit one-on-one with an expert who would interpret the meaning of their answers.

Laura's outcome was profound. She thought she wanted to be a teacher, but the test showed that she was very good in marketing, sales, and business, and that she should stay away from sciences. That was helpful to her because she didn't like sciences or the science as she knew it in high school. The results were quite valuable as a student and shaped how she thought about her life. She felt confident knowing she was good in certain areas and that she should stay away from other areas. If she ever thought of going into business and sales, that could be something she could be strong in.

Isn't it ironic that she enrolled at university to be a teacher and discovered that wasn't what she imagined she wanted to be? After she had gone halfway through the year, she transferred into a science program to train for massage therapy. She loved the anatomy part of science and became a registered massage therapist. While she isn't in business per se, her inclination to marketing and sales helped her as an entrepreneur.

Family is still important. The kids and grandkids used to vote on where they wanted to go for Christmas holidays. We used to go up to the Great Lakes to the cottage and go on sleigh rides. But they all vote for Florida now that they're living in North Carolina. Their argument is they don't have clothes to go north, and they all love Florida.

We have large closets in every bedroom. We put air mattresses in them, so it's like a grandkid's own private little room. The house sleeps fourteen. We have a good time and go on lots of adventures. All year long, the kids go hard on their schedules, so at Christmas, they just like to relax in the pool and go boating, which is right up my alley.

Our granddaughters often spend school breaks with us. They bring their friends, and they all have fun together. They love it, and we love having them. We're a ten-minute walk to the beach. We go boating. We sit around our pool. Marilyn makes dinner, and they don't rush off. They sit around the table and talk and talk. Being able to host the girls is one of the big reasons Marilyn has learned to love Florida.

We have open hearts and an open home. The home we live in may not be the final one we purchase, but it is a fine place to offer hospitality and generosity while enjoying a fulfilling retirement.

Chapter 17, Retirement

Retirement is a major life transition that can be viewed as a reward for years of hard work. Retirement can also bring about stress, anxiety, and depression among other mental health impacts. Only a few months (and for some, a few days) into retirement is all it takes for the novelty of being on "permanent vacation" to start to wear off. You miss the sense of identity, meaning, and purpose that came with your job, the structure it gave your days, or the social aspect of having co-workers. It's important to know that you're not just retiring from something, but to something.

- As you think of retirement, what are some new sources of meaning or activities that can enrich your life?
- Are there any you give back and continue to enrich other people's lives?

18

KEYNOTE TO THE WORLD

DO YOU KNOW HOW IT FEELS TO BE IN OVER YOUR HEAD AND regret saying yes to what you thought was a wonderful opportunity, and now can only hope it will not kill you? I said yes to Harold and Darlene Albrecht.

Harold owned a private dental practice in the Kitchener region for twenty-seven years, founded a church, and served the Kitchener-Conestoga riding as a Member of Parliament for thirteen years. I got to know him after he became an MP. His wife, Darlene, filled the role of Executive Director of the Christian Embassy of Canada, an organization that seeks to inspire and connect members of Parliament, senators, ambassadors, diplomats, and business leaders to help them better achieve their mandates and to resource them as leaders.

An annual Christmas dinner is the highlight of their year. The evening allows busy leaders and their spouses to relax, network, and enjoy special music and meaningful reminders of the season. Diplomats appreciate what is often a first opportunity to experience Canadian Christmas traditions.

In 2017, 186 diplomats, parliamentarians, and business leaders, representing 56 nations, accepted an invitation to attend the dinner. Leaders from various backgrounds were invited to participate in readings, reflections, and seasonal music. There is always a keynote address. Darlene inquired if I would be willing to keynote that year's dinner. It was an honor. I said yes. Marilyn was happy because she would need a new dress suitable for such an event.

I did what I always do: pray, start to prepare my talk, and then, in a bit of a panic, call my friend Ken Taylor and said, "Help." I did that more than once in the weeks leading up to the dinner. Ken is an exceptional public speaker and an even better coach. He read through what I had written, offered feedback and support, and tried unsuccessfully to lighten my anxiety by joking about some of his speaking faux pas.

Iron sharpens iron, so a friend sharpens a friend.
— Proverbs 27:17 (NIV)

My anxiety arose from wanting to ensure I didn't say anything offensive, given the mix of different religious traditions and backgrounds in the room. At the same time, I wanted to communicate something that would respect the Christmas story. I sweated profusely while preparing my speech, revising it repeatedly.

The dinner began well. We met the high commissioner for the Republic of Uganda, H.E. Joy Ruth Acheng; the high commissioner for the Republic of Cyprus, H.E. Pavlos Anastasiades; the ambassador of the Republic of Zimbabwe, Dean of the Diplomatic Corps, H.E. Florence Chideya; the ambassador of the Republic of Honduras, H.E. Sofia Cerrato Rodriguez; the high commissioner for Jamaica, H.E. Janice Avonne Miller; and the ambassador of the Republic of Hungary, H.E. Bálint Odor.

Marilyn and I were seated with the ambassador from Vietnam. As we were introduced, I felt grateful for the way God had orchestrated the seating plan and for every day I had spent in the ambassador's country. We had an intriguing conversation about Magnussen's international trade ventures in Vietnam. He showed genuine interest in our warehouse design and the standards we used to employ and provide for Vietnamese workers. This conversation distracted me from the quickly approaching moment when I would be introduced.

Darlene had the honor of welcoming and introducing me. Listening to her made me want to meet the man she was describing. Marilyn gave me a smile and a thumbs-up as I left my seat to walk towards the platform. My memory took me back to the little kid sweeping floors in his dad's shop. He could never have envisioned the journey that would bring him to a moment like this.

I offered a silent prayer for God's help while walking across the platform to the sounds of applause suited to the occasion.

My talk began by explaining how humbled Marilyn and I felt being entrusted with the honor of making their acquaintances and the pleasure of addressing them.

"Tonight, I want to share some personal thoughts on a key leadership virtue at the heart of the Christmas story, the birth of Jesus. There is a way of living out our lives that will, among other things, elevate our skills as leaders, enable us to know healthy, happy relationships with others, help us experience a strong and intimate marriage, and birth in us a deep, confident, inner strength."

I had Ken to thank for a confident introduction which I read and re-read countless times. Faces in the audience told me I had their interest.

> *The Christmas story, the story of the birth of the son of God, the birth of the greatest human who has ever lived, that event vividly displays this virtue. It seems as if every element in the account of the birth of Jesus whispers this word.*

The virtue I wanted these leaders to focus on was humility.

> *God chose a poor teenage girl, living in a far-flung corner of the Roman Empire to be the mother of Jesus. Jesus is born, not in a palace, but in a barn. The announcement of his birth isn't made to ambassadors and other government officials, but to a group of shepherds, outcasts who live a nomadic life on the fringe of society. Joseph and Mary are so poor that the sacrifice they bring to the temple, in gratitude for Jesus' birth, is reserved for those living below the poverty line. He is raised in obscurity in a tiny village and learns from his father the trade of a common laborer.*

> *But it isn't just his birthplace or the occupation that echoes the word 'humility' in the life of Jesus. In Matthew 11:28, in the Bible, Jesus describes himself. He says, "Let me teach you, because I am humble and gentle at heart, and you will find rest for your souls."*

> *Think of the art, the architecture, the music, the books, and the billions of people who follow him. Even our calendars have changed and been reset BC/AD by his birth. And at his heart is humility. The older I get, the more I have come to realize the power and strength true humility can bring into one's life.*

I shared my life story, beginning with my dad's little cabinetmaking business in a chicken coop. How at the age of twenty I started working full-time with him, worrying I might be bored, and never imagining that Magnussen Furniture would grow into an international enterprise, all the while trusting God as my partner.

"I have been far from perfect, but I can tell you that learning to listen to God was the wisest decision I have ever made." I ventured on, sharing how some people I have interacted with have the impression that the Bible is not relevant. The book is full of wisdom and worth checking out.

"Business is all about people, and people are all about relationships, and people are drawn to honest values, and in particular, people are drawn to humility."

I shared the lessons I learned about integrity and told the stories of stealing designs from American manufacturers and then making amends. They heard about the blessings and challenges that come with a family-owned enterprise; going to the brink of bankruptcy by being over-leveraged when the economy suddenly went south; the incredible growth to 3,000 customers worldwide, with distributions centers in Vietnam and California, and 300 team members managing 10,000 plus contracted workers globally; the pleasure of seeing a succession plan result in an ever-increasing footprint, innovation, and profitability. God was my partner every step of the way and He deserved all the credit for anything that sounded like success.

To tie it all together, I told the story of the timely settlement of an old lawsuit with a dollar amount exactly equal to the amount needed to secure our financial position. "There is no doubt in my mind that God had orchestrated a miracle. He used the tough times to teach us a lesson about pride, and the need for us to humble ourselves and let him be the leader. God has been the one blessing us."

My talk closed with the declarations,

> *I am a follower of Jesus Christ. I have learned so many lessons through my simple faith in the humble Jesus of the Christmas story. Over the years I would celebrate the business success, and personally take the credit, but today after seeing my career playing out, I know that Jesus is the real hero.*
>
> *Jesus "took the humble position of a slave and was born as a human being. When he appeared in human form, he humbled himself in obedience to God and died a criminal's death on a cross. Therefore, God elevated him to the place of highest honor and gave him the name above all other*

names, that at the name of Jesus every knee should bow, in heaven and on earth and under the earth, and every tongue declare that Jesus Christ is Lord, to the glory of God the Father" (Philippians 2:6-11 (NLT)).

The response after a talk should always be greater than the reception preceding a talk. Darlene shared her appreciation, and the standing ovation affirmed her sentiment. Marilyn and the Vietnamese ambassador assured me I had done well.

Now I could enjoy my dessert.

Chapter 18, Keynote to the World

Imagine you have an audience of influential people.

- What would you tell them about your life? What stories would you share?
- What principles and qualities would you share from your life as the means of your success?

19

THE LAST WORD

STEVE JOBS IS ASSOCIATED WITH AN AMBITION TO PUT A dent in the universe. Jobs was aware that his company was doing something significant. Apple's work could influence the future of the world.

My universe is Magnussen. First the Magnussen family. Then the company. I expect my faith in God to make a dent in that universe.

More than 200 times a second, someone is googling questions about God— questions like, "Is God real?" We want to know if God really is real, and if He is real, does He really care about us? If God is real, why is there suffering? If there is a God, why doesn't He make Himself obvious?

What happens after death?

I need to show my kids how to die well.

One of our acquaintances turned sixty. He was at an age where he surpassed any of his family. His father and brother died young. Sixty isn't old, but he says he is worried about dying. The days are long, but the years are short.

At the time of writing this book, I am seventy-three years old. The days go slow, but the years go fast. There is more to life than our earthly existence. We are spirits in a body who live forever, either with our Creator or separated from our Creator. I want to spend eternity with my Creator.

I have full confidence and faith in Jesus Christ as my Savior, who died in my place and rose from the dead so that I have everlasting life through Him.

I was assigned a book to read in high school, The Adventures of Tom Saw-yer. Tom and Huckleberry Finn, both presumed dead, walk into the middle of their funeral service. I've often thought of that. I would love to be a fly on the wall at my funeral service but I'm not willing to fake it to see what happens. Marilyn and I occasionally talk about death and funerals. I want mine to be upbeat. I don't want it to be too draggy. I want a memorial service that exalts Jesus and gives people reason for hope and faith.

Death is not a period at the end of life's sentence.

Death is a comma that punctuates life to an eternal level.

All my choices, imperfect as they are, were made in devotion to Jesus.

An associate of mine was diagnosed with cancer. She didn't look at God as being hard on her or unfaithful to her. She said, "God could heal me, but he may choose not to. I trust God." I never heard anything negative come out of her mouth. She had a cup-half-full attitude. I want to be known for being a cup-half-full believer because I have hope.

I get corrected in my spirit when I want to be negative about something. And that doesn't mean that you don't talk about facts and real-life situations. But you talk about them with a backdrop of trust in God.

Cry out for insight and ask for understanding. Search for them as you would for silver; seek them like hidden treasures. Then you will understand what it means to fear the Lord, and you will gain knowledge of God. For the Lord grants wisdom. From his mouth come knowledge and understanding. He grants a treasure of common sense to the honest. He is a shield to those who walk with integrity. He guards the paths of the just and protects those who are faithful to him.
— Proverbs 2:3-8 (NLT)

I have been asked three profound questions:

- How do I cope with suffering and adversity?
- What is my interpretation of death?
- Have I made preparations for my own death?

The dash on a tombstone, symbolizing the time between birth and death, is remarkably short. Life unfolds rapidly. However, one can be well-prepared. This preparation stems from the knowledge and confidence that Jesus is exactly who he claimed to be. This understanding makes a world of difference.

We are all aware that death is inevitable. Preparation entails living life to the fullest extent possible. If I fall ill or meet with an accident that ends my life, people will undoubtedly know that I'll be reveling in a superior place with God. Hopefully, there will be a handful of people who mourn the loss. But their mourning should be limited, perhaps only missing my presence and the interruptions I caused. Death is a certainty. No one gets out of here alive, and no one leaves with a U-Haul.

I think back to when I broke my neck. The doctor said, "You're not taking this seriously." I've often reflected on his comment. I did take the injury seriously, but I think it was my faith that kept me from being anxious about living with a broken neck. I wasn't overwhelmed by it, nor did I take my recovery for granted. Every time I see someone in a wheelchair who is paralyzed from the neck down, I think, That could have been me. But I believe that for some reason, nothing to do with me, God spared my life and healed my neck. Many other times, I thought, Lord, is this going to be the end; I leave it with you, and it wasn't the end. It became the beginning of bigger and greater things.

When I suffered that neck injury, Marilyn and I confronted it with unwavering faith, secure in the belief that God was with us. The injury was critical. It could have resulted in a torn spinal cord and paralysis. Initially, I was somewhat irritated. However, God showed mercy to me, not because of any merit on my part. I witnessed a miracle and have since lived each day with gratitude, basking in the light of God's benevolence.

In 2008, our business appeared to be teetering on the edge of bankruptcy. I reassured our boys, "If we get shut down and the business fails, God has a superior plan. We need to pray, work diligently, and strive for a turnaround." With an exceptional team and wisdom, we managed to reverse our fortunes swiftly. We came to the realization and conclusion that God is in control. This is our approach to adversity.

Becoming a believer in Jesus Christ impacts life so much that I can't imagine life without faith in Jesus. I became a Christian through a childhood prayer of confession, believing that God would forgive a kid like me. I remain a Christian because the evidence is so compelling that Jesus really is the one-

and-only Son of God who proved his divinity by rising from the dead. That meant following him was the most rational and logical step I could possibly take. That kind of faith works.

There is a reality and clarity to an authentic faith in God, but Christian faith often gets a bad rap. Christians and churches haven't done a lot to dispel that reputation. Christianity consists of more than Sunday morning go to church and a bunch of religious rules. That's what confused and disappointed my dad. Some of the rules Christian churches have build walls and not bridges to God. They dissuade people from pursuing a relationship with God.

All other religions are about doing enough good to outweigh the bad. I don't know of anybody I've talked to about Jesus that doesn't say something like, "I'm just trying to do the best I can. If there is a God, he's going to accept me based on the good I've done." Doing the best you can doesn't work. Magnussens are known for their rigorous work ethic. We're trained to be achievers. In our family, responsible people work for what they want. However, a strong work ethic doesn't work either in a walk with God.

Success in life is how you walk with God.

Success is not measured monetarily; it's having enough wealth to cover your expenses and to be a blessing to your first and second and third generations. It's not about dying with the most toys.

Success is being thankful for the path that you chose, even though you weren't perfect.

Success is reflecting on the impact that God had on all the things that happened in your life.

Success is looking back on your life with the assurance you did the best you could with what you were given.

Success is seeing what God has done and how he's gotten you through trials.

God brought our family into healthy and loving relationships based on true respect. He looked after the details out of our control, and we learned we control nothing more than our attitude. He protected us and gave us wisdom. We made decisions based on faith, and we saw how they all played out for good.

God showed up in so many ways. Our family had some bumps along the way, but we stood together. That doesn't mean we escaped challenges and health issues, but God brought us through them. Now, thanks to God, our grandchildren are an incredible blessing to us. Success is seeing them growing in life and faith in Jesus, and shows me that I have, hopefully, made a dent for

Jesus in my Magnussen universe.

But in the end, finishing well with Jesus is true success. And nobody can go bigger than that.

God so loved the world [that includes you] that he gave his one and only Son, that whoever believes in him shall not perish but have eternal life.
—John 3:16 (NIV)

Here is a simple prayer for you to trust God for forgiveness and life:

Lord Jesus, I know that I am a sinner, and I ask for Your forgiveness. I believe You died for my sins and rose from the dead. I turn from my sins and invite You to come into my life. I want to trust and follow You as my Lord and Savior. Thank you.

If this simple memoir influenced you to pray that prayer and follow Jesus, I truly will have made a dent in the universe.

Thank you for reading.

Go Big!

Chapter 19, The Last Word

Facing death is a challenge that everyone will face at some point. It can be a difficult time, but it can also be a meaningful and rewarding experience, a time to reflect on the life we've lived.

- If you were a fly on the wall at your own funeral, what do you think people would say about you?
- How do you cope with suffering and adversity?
- What is your interpretation of death?
- Have you made preparations for my own death?
- How do you define success? Finish this sentence, several times if necessary: Success is ...
- Where do you see God showing up in your life?

MY FATHER'S STORY

This memoir was inspired by my father's biography.

My sister was the custodian of our dad's keepsakes, one of which was a thirteen-page, handwritten manuscript of his life story, penned in 1985. She gave Marilyn and me a photocopy, which we read but soon misplaced and forgot about. A decade later, Marilyn suggested we get another copy from my sister and distribute it to all the kids for Christmas.

When Laura read what Dad had written, she exclaimed, "We have to read this to the grandkids." She discovered fascinating aspects of Grandpa's life that she had never known. After finishing high school, Laura wanted to trace his roots, so her graduation gift was a trip to Germany to visit the places he often spoke about. She was thrilled with his written record.

On Christmas Day 2022, Laura gathered all fourteen of us in our living room in Naples and began to read. She's a skilled reader and did an excellent job emphasizing the dramatic parts of Grandpa's story. I looked around the room at the kids, and they were captivated by her reading. Every so often, she would pause, and they'd exclaim, "Can you believe that he went to New York City and they tried to con him? Can you believe this?" I thought they would be getting up, fetching water, or going to the bathroom, but they just sat there, engrossed. They learned so many things about my dad that they never knew. There were even facts that I had forgotten.

Immediately following the reading, Laura enthusiastically suggested, "Dad, you should write your story." Marilyn and the rest echoed their support. I wasn't as enthusiastic. Who would want to read my story?

What you've just read is the result of my family's tenacious persistence. My story would be incomplete without my dad's story. As you read what he wrote and compare it with what I wrote, you'll notice some discrepancies regarding dates and numbers. That's more a result of faded memories than disagreement over facts. You will also notice shifts between past, present, and future. Dad was still thinking ahead, planning for the future of Magnussen.

Enjoy.

AUTOBIOGRAPHY OF INGWER MAGNUSSEN

It all started from 1929 to 1933. Canada was in a deep depression. Many people out of work offered themselves to work for 10 cents per hour at that time. We had no unemployment insurance, social security benefits, and no old age pension either. Everybody was on their own.

I was 23 years old, and no parents to go to for shelter. I left them behind in Germany in 1929 at an age of 19 years.

I had, however, saved $365.00, which I could use for one year room and board, or take a chance and start a furniture business at a time when many large and small furniture factories went out of business. But that was the chance I was willing to take.

But now I am a little ahead of my story and will start at the beginning.

I am one of six children: two boys and four girls. My father was a postman. My mother was busy looking after us. I was born on the 12th of March, 1909, in a very small village named Klixbüll, in Nordfriesland in the northern part of Germany near the North Sea and Danish border. It was a red brick, one-story house with a straw-covered roof, with living quarters at one end of the house. An entrance floor and storage were separating the stall from the living quarters. Hay and straw pushed into the attic kept the house nice and cozy in the winter, cool in the summer, and would feed the animals in the winter.

In 1911, when I was two years of age, we all moved to the city of Flensburg—a 3-hour train ride East from here, right on the East Sea near the harbor where I could see ships from our elevated back yard.

Three years later, in 1914, World War I broke out. We all had to tighten our belts. At the end of the war in 1918, which we lost, my Father also lost all his savings; in fact, everybody else lost their bank accounts, because the money became worthless. It was cheaper to light a cigar with a 1,000 Mark bill than to use a match.

The same happened after the 2nd World War.

In 1917, I had to leave home at the age of eight, because of the shortage of food.

I was sent to the city of Husum to strangers. The man had three grown-up children and was a self-employed butcher. *There should be no shortage of food in this house,* I thought. I was treated as their own, especially the grown-up girls were kind to me; however, the boy, at that time going to the university, treated me a little rough. I think he was a little jealous because he was the youngest boy and was getting a little less attention on account of me.

One time I went along with him in a horse and buggy out of town. There he had to get off and left me alone with the horse and buggy. As I was always curious by nature, I wondered what would happen if I should just by accident pull on the reins, and in the back of my mind I would just like just a little distance between him and me. He noticed me just in time and came running after me as I had never seen him running before. Finally, he jumped on the buggy and preached to me all the way home.

I stayed in Husum half a year and even went to school there. The only connection I had with my parents was by mail.

In 1918, at nine years of age, the food shortage was getting worse. This time I was sent to Denmark, a long, long way up North. I came to a farmer just outside the city of Vejle. To get there we boarded a water-wheel steamboat—large wheels on each side brought the boat in motion. We had one rough day, and the boat was tossed from one side to the other. A line spread across the center kept us from running from one side to the other to avoid accelerating the motion.

Finally arriving at the Port of Vejle, we gathered in a large reception room. There must have been hundreds of children and their foster parents. All children had their identification in front of them, and in this manner our foster parents could identify us. But the problem with this was that everybody had me turn around to see the name plate, which really interfered with munching all that wonderful food and hot chocolate. I decided to turn the nameplate around my back for easy access and to prevent further interference with my meal.

Finally, my foster parents discovered me and remarked about the way of my sign and the ingenuity of the nameplate reversal. However, I could not understand one word they were saying. For half a year, they treated me as their own and bought me clothing and toys, especially boats they knew I liked so much, because I spent so much time at the brook—damming up water and building bridges. I really had a good time and the language barrier did not seem to matter much—love took its place.

For every egg I collected from all over the barn and yard, I received one cent. I found eggs in holes that they could never have reached before. They must have been a month old, but the price was still the same—one cent.

Again, the only contact that I had with my parents was by mail.

When I returned to Flensburg, Germany, my father greeted me at the railroad station. I spoke to him in Danish, saying, "Dad, I thought the train should come from the other side"—but who cares? I was in my father's arms, and that was all that mattered.

We were real pals. We would walk together a lot, picking coal from scrap hills, and gathering firewood from dead branches in the forest to heat our kitchen, where we spent most of the time, because it was the warmest place.

Walking through the streets with my Father, watching construction and furniture factories, he would always hint mildly to me, "Someday, you will have your own business."

At the age of 14, I was confirmed at the Lutheran Church in Flensburg in 1923, and I had to wear "long pants" for the first time in my life. I felt foolish and looked to the right and to the left before I walked out of the door—making sure nobody was around.

But in good time I got used to it. Now I was a man! But I still like to dream!

I liked to work with wood and in my teenage years I made dollhouses and furniture to fit into the dollhouses for my sisters. Finally, I was promoted to an all-around house fixer. Whenever anything was wrong, they called on me whether it was plumbing or electrical work, painting or masonry work.

Behind our house, we had a high, steep hill, and the water would keep washing down the earth. Throughout my training years, from ages 4 to 18, I took on the job of building walls and 40 to 50 cement steps up the steep hill. I also improved our little lookout house on top of the bank, which had a beautiful view of the harbour—watching the boats coming in and going out. The only problem was the labour-consuming time it took to bring food and drinks to this high altitude.

The wheels in my head started spinning. What can be done? My motto, was then already as it is now: "The impossible we do right away and the miraculous takes a little longer."

I ended up stringing a pulley-line with a basket attached to the kitchen window of our house. My mother would fill the basket with food and we would turn a handle to wind it up. A real labor-saving device!

At 14 years of age, I decided to learn a trade. Furniture appealed to me. There was no opening in small furniture shops where one could learn the trade, and in four years receive a diploma to be a full-fledged tradesman.

Instead, I went to the *Kunstgewerbliche Fach Schule,* which means "Technical Arts School" in English. There I learned everything pertaining to making furniture from the bottom up. First, we had to do everything by hand, using hand-planes, drill, chisel, etc.

A whole boxful of tools hanging on the wall was provided for each student, and also a real woodworking bench.

It was exciting, especially when we saw stools develop in front of our eyes. I really enjoyed the four years of apprenticeship.

We also learned drafting, making blueprints, designing, and of course, bookkeeping and calculating. In fact, everything pertaining to the furniture business, if you should desire to start your own.

But it was quite a sacrifice to my parents. Instead of making money and paying room and board, I had four years full room and board, besides it cost 20 Deutsche Mark a month to pay for the schooling, but it paid off.

I received four letters of recognition and accomplishment, and three money prizes in competition to be the first. It really came easy to me because I liked it.

Sometimes I was so taken up with a job that I didn't hear the bell ringing and everybody leaving. Finally, the teacher came to me, tapped me on the shoulder and said, "Don't you want to go home to eat?"

Easter 1928, I finished trade school and received a document with "Extra Good."

After I left school, I got a job right away in the small town of Hademarschen. My recommendation from the school helped because jobs were scarce. A year later I left on my own accord and worked further south of Germany in Guerslow, on recommendation of a fellow worker.

We were laid off for a short period of time at Christmas, and I went home by train, a 5-hour ride. Here I decided to go to America. My brother, already in America, advised me against it, and said that I might end up polishing shoes in New York. So, I decided that is what I would do if it became necessary and applied for my Visa.

In the meantime, I visited most of my relatives within a 100-mile radius by train. Here I learned from a friend that a certain Mr. Bahnen from Waterloo, Canada was visiting his sister living in the country. I contacted him by mail—sent my diploma with four letters of recognition to him in Germany, and on the strength of that was promised a job at The Globe Furniture Co. in Waterloo. That meant I didn't have to start at the bottom of the ladder by polishing shoes. Now I could relax, and the rest of the waiting time I spent doing odd jobs at home.

This was the time that the city of Flensburg received a radio sender [transmitter] in the form of a high tower. Everybody was busy buying and installing crystal sets—very inexpensive.

This was the time when Hitler and the Communists were working hard getting prospect votes. It was about a 50-50 deal, and we didn't know for sure whether Communist or Fascists would take over. Nevertheless, I built a crystal set, and installed it in our living room, kitchen, my bedroom, and Grandmother's room, by way of wires, but only one crystal set. Every night I would go to bed with my earphones on and listened to sweet music and fell asleep, with my earphones beside me the next morning. There was no static at all.

My grandmother would spin on a spinning wheel with earphones over her ear. All she had to do was to plug the cord into the wall socket. What a contrast of old and new.

That was about the time I left for U.S.A. It was May 20, 1929 that I left on the ship "Deutschland" from Hamburg. My mother & father were standing on the pier, I was leaning over the boat railing, the band was playing "Nun ade due mein liebe feimatland" meaning in English, "Goodbye my beloved Homeland." It was very touching. All eyes filled with tears, and the question was, "When will we meet again?"

My mother and father waved to me smiling, with tears in their eyes. They, too, wondered, "When will we meet again?"

I was 19 years old and soon war measures began. Corresponding would stop, and as it turned out, I would never see my father again. The first letter after the war had a black edge around it. I was afraid to open it, fearing it announced my father's death. I had always hoped that he would come to visit me in Canada and enjoy my business with me, as he was so instrumental in it. I didn't mind stringing along, but at the end I would have liked to share it with him. My mother, also my four sisters, I saw on my first trip to Germany after the War.

But now I am getting ahead of myself, and want to continue my trip. We arrived in New York on the 27th of May 1929, with $25.00 in our pocket; this was compulsory. We also had a big sign with a number on our pallet to identify us. Special police in plain clothing were assigned to watch those newcomers.

We were waiting for a bus to take us to the railway station for further transportation. I was to go to my uncle and aunt in Boon, Iowa, and this is where I made my biggest mistake. I took off my safety sign because I didn't want to be a little boy walking around with a sign in front of me. I was too big for that, and this was the result: soon a German-speaking man came up to me and talked real nice, and as he was doing so he took the last evidence from my pallet, namely, the pin to which the sign was attached. Finally, he said, "We don't have to wait for a bus, we can take a taxi," and so we did. I began to feel uneasy. *Where is he going to take me?* He, in turn, showed me the city, explained this and that.

All I realized is that I had made the biggest mistake in my life and became alert, almost like a watchdog.

He must have felt it, or it was an angel watching over me. He ended up taking me to the railway station and let me put my belongings into the locker. I was on edge all the time, looking for police just in case. Finally, he said, after standing there a considerable length of time, "I am going back," and asked me for the taxi money.

Against my best judgment I gave him the money for the taxi both ways just to get rid of him. Afterwards I asked myself why would he go out of his way, take his time, just to take me to the railroad station, when the bus would have done for nothing. He was up to something and had a change of heart. I should have known better; we were warned in Germany against boy and girl snatchers.

I had the same experience in Hamburg, Germany. In public school we were already warned that teenagers in my age group, 19 years, were in great demand in the French Legionnaires Army in Africa, and a handsome bounty (money) was offered to anyone that would catch one.

I was alone in the big city, more or less just loafing and buying ice cream. Someone must have watched me for some time and finally came up to me speaking friendly. Then he suggested to go to a tavern for a drink, but he did not suggest the nearest place on the main street. No, he wanted to go to the back alley tavern, where perhaps he had made arrangement with someone for a small fee to put a drug into my drink. Presto! Unconscious, I would end up as a French Legionnaire in Africa. Wouldn't that have been something? After all my education, I would be forced to kill people. I am sure that wasn't 'my cup of tea.' I saw through him, thanks to previous public school education, declined his offer, and said, "Ice cream and drinks don't mix."

Coming back to New York, I was waiting and wondering, *Is this the right station?* and *When are the others coming?* Soon I saw some familiar faces trickling in, and after finding out my departure of the train, I was relaxed. Since I had plenty of time, I left the station and toured the city within walking distance, when I noticed such lovely big red apples. I couldn't speak English, so I just pointed to the apples. I bought one for 5 cents. The big high skyscraper I had never seen before astounded me, and at the corner I kept looking up, up, up. Soon I had others looking also, but nobody knew exactly what they were looking for—and I couldn't tell them on account of the language barrier. Finally, I boarded the train surrounded by friends from the boat.

One girl from Hungary I would have liked to get married to, but I was too young.

A student going in for the ministry could talk a little German and when he heard me saying, "Donnerwetter noch einmal," he thought that I was swearing. and said that I should not use such language, but in defense I said that it only meant, "Thunderstorm."

Arriving in Boon, a small town, I walked down the street with my suitcase, to where my uncle lived. He didn't know exactly when I was coming, and telephoning never entered my mind, since I never used one before, and would not know how to operate one. Finally, I arrived. My uncle was a brother of my father. His wife, somewhat taller, wore the pants, you might say. One time at a meal I complained that the soup was too hot. Without hesitation she said, "Why don't you take your bowl and walk around the house until it has cooled off?" I looked at her, and without hesitation, I said, "I will exactly do that." With that I walked out the door and did exactly what she said, and the soup was ready to eat on my return.

In a way I am a little joker too, and if I could make people laugh, I would do it, but I can't remember whether my aunt laughed or not. She might have thought, *What do the neighbors think of having a crazy nephew walking a bowl of soup around the house?*

Now that my destination was Canada, I had to get a special passport for Canada. It took about a month, but finally I got a letter from Ottawa allowing me to enter. And once more "goodbye" to my uncle and aunt and many other friends I had made there.

My uncle later lost all his life's savings in the 1933 bank crash and died a poor man.

I left for Canada by train: Waterloo was my destination, and the address of Mr. Bahnsen, the Manager of the Globe Furniture was given to me. I arrived at the Waterloo station, a station that nobody used at that time. Everybody got off in Kitchener and used the streetcar on rails with a clink-clonk sound to Waterloo. I didn't know that and after two hours of waiting at the Kitchener railway I finally arrived at the small station in Waterloo. I was the only passenger, with a lot of milk cans and freight. The surroundings did not look inviting. All I saw was dumpy backyards of stores facing King Street in Waterloo. I walked up to King Street and got a taxi, since I didn't know where Mr. Bahnsen lived. Later I found out from King Street to Albert Street, near the old fire hall, was only 5-10 minute walk.

Mr. Bahnsen and his wife invited me for dinner, and for the first few weeks took me out a lot of weekends in their car—that was something.

He also took me to the factory, Globe Furniture, just off Erb Street. In the meantime, my large container had arrived with all my tools.

Later I made a toolbox and hung it on the wall near my workbench. The foreman, a German, got me a boarding place for $5.00 a week, also German speaking. At the factory, we were making mostly church furniture. Once I helped setting up richly carved furniture in a cathedral in London, Ontario. It took about a month or more to install. But within two years, depression caused us to lose our jobs. I was making 40 cents per hour when I left and started one and a half years before with 35 cents per hour, 10 hours a day, for 5 days, and Saturday 5 hours—55 hours per week and $24.75 weekly take-home pay. Income Tax hadn't been invented yet—that came later!

The Bank would pay 3% Interest, with $5.00 taken off for room and board, leaving me with $19.75 net. A pound of butter was 20 cents; a large three-scoop of ice cream was 5 cents.

After I left Globe Furniture, I started working for Hentschel Furniture. The owner had also worked for Globe Furniture and, when laid off, started a business for himself. He had a business in Germany. He was middle-aged, married, and had two children, a boy and a girl, about 9 to 12 years of age. I enjoyed the work, but money was scarce, and I started accepting IOUs from him.

I also took time off to make a folding boat, 14 ft. long. It was collapsible and in 10 minutes, I could take it apart, go down the Grand River from Bridgeport, and be picked up by bus in Freeport, carrying the parts in two handsome bags.

The hull was water-proof canvas, brown in color, with a white top. I painted a white swan on each side of the front of the boat and had a lot of fun in the park, taking boys and girls for a ride upstream past the railway bridge until a lack of water brought our journey to an end. Each had a double paddle, which I made out of 1" pine wood. When collapsed, the boat was only 5' long, fitting into a nice bag.

But then one day the fun stopped. A smart boy—son of a hot dog businessman on King Street selling foot-long hot dogs for 10 cents—changed it all. This is what he said to me: "You should make a business out of renting your boat out and make money." And that's where the fun stopped. I made no money and lost my friends.

When Hentschel owed me $400.00, I said to him that I could not afford to pay $6.00 room and board, and work for nothing. So, we arranged to take it out in room and board. This gave me a lot of free time.

I went two nights a week to the K-W high school to learn English for new Canadians. Later, I learned Business English and Grammar in a Canadian class at night. Here I found our lady teacher in English and Grammar extremely good. I took private lessons once a week, paying her $2.00 for a half hour, which was in those days extremely high. At that time garbage collectors made more than some of the teachers. I got enough homework to keep me busy six to eight hours a day all week, besides taking violin lessons and practicing. It kept me going. But each day at 4 o'clock I said to myself, "Enough is enough. There is more in life than work alone." I picked up my skates and walked from William Street to the Waterloo Park, skating and always investing 5 cents on an Oh Henry chocolate bar. (The skating was free.)

I came to know a group of boys and girls having fun at suppertime. We said, "Goodbye, until we meet again the next day."

In the summer I would put up my pup tent beside the house and had a lot of fun with small groups of boys and girls, including the Hentschel children. This reminds me of an incident 15 years later when I had my own business and purchased some items at the Weber Hardware Co., a fine young man came up to me and said, "Do you remember me? You and I used to sit at the sidewalk curb and you were telling me bedtime stories." He must have been about 4 or

5 years old then. It really pleased me to hear that.

I usually went out with boys younger than I, climbing trees in the bush until the top end of the tree would bend down, and we landed safely on the ground. My pup tent and boat we used for camping once at the Hamilton Bay, before pollution changed all that. Mr. Hentschel had another boarder and the six of us at one meal had to share one small can of sardines, costing 5 to 10 cents a can.

Broken windows were plugged up with a rag until money was available to buy glass. At times like this I always liked to have a friend that worked in a bakery or butcher shop, and a little visit would always pay off because I was always hungry.

In 1933, when Mr. Hentschel and I had settled our financial matters, I said to myself, "I think that I can do better myself," and left. I was then 25 or 26 years old. It was in 1933. I looked around for a building where I could live and work. I came across a shack—once a horse or chicken stable, 50 feet long and 14 feet wide. The one wall was ripped down for firewood, leaving the 2 x 4 standing. Also, one end was well on its way to being wrecked. The wooden floor was completely stripped. People living nearby used the boards for firewood. After one looked at it, I realized that I could take it down and make a building half the size out of it, and put in a new floor, and electric lights. It would be a good beginning.

So I went to the owner, whom I knew, and offered him $20 in cash and I would take the building away. He laughed at me and thought I was joking about the price. So I invited him to see for himself what was left. I said, "In another winter there won't be anything left." He saw the light and gave it to me for $20.

And I saw the light too in a fine building half the size with new coat of Redwood stain, shining in the sunlight in front of me. This was to be my first building of which I became the proud owner, but I am a little ahead of myself.

First, I had to have a place to put it. I knew Mr. Pagel that had a hatchery business along the side of the bridge on Bridgeport Road. We made a deal. I would pay him $2.00 a month rent for putting the building on his lot and buying all the eggs I needed from him wholesale.

Now came the hard work of dismantling and putting the building together again, single-handed, with a little help here and there. The good wall I sawed into four sections with a handsaw and loaded them onto a truck, along with the two end parts. The roof boards and floor joists had to be taken apart, and piece by piece, and loaded onto the truck. On the new lot I reversed the ordeal and in two months of hard work became the proud owner of a red-stained building with a green roof, new floor, and tile chimney. The electric I had put in for $35.00.

In one 6′ by 4′ corner, I had my living quarters. The bed took a space of 6′ x 2′, 2′ x 2′ for the table, 2′ x 2′ for the closet, and 2′ x 2′ space to walk around on. The cupboards for dishes I built next to it in the shop.

I traded a small 12-14″ bandsaw and a 6″ planer machine for two work-benches that I didn't have to deliver until one year later. I had previously bought a small circular saw with drill attachment.

Now I was ready for business. My cost of living had gone down from $6.00 a week to $2.00 a week, and with the $2.00 a month rent for the land, I would say my expenses were low. I had already contacted two firms that would give me the business: Dick the Upholsterer and Mr. Hamel – Luxury Upholstering. At one time I had an order for 12 chesterfield frames, along with 24 chair frames without legs and show-wood. They came in a set of three—one chesterfield and two chair frames for $5.00. I figured the material was one part, labor and overhead was one part, and one part was profit. In other words, for every dollar that I spent on material I would get $2.00 for labor and overhead. Since the overhead was low, and I supplied the labor, the $2.00 was my own. Multiply this by 12 sets, I could live for three months on that order.

I was in this building for one and a half to two years and had bought $500 worth of machines as follows: surface planer, double spindle shaper, large 30″ bandsaw, 14-16″ jointer, drum and desk sander, swing cut-off saw, etc. These machines I had stored in an old building, free of charge. The only problem was, the roof was leaking, and the machines got wet whenever it rained, so I had to cover them up, and oiled all the bare metal parts to keep them from rusting.

In 1935, after one and a half to two years, the place was getting too small, and I moved to the former gas-work building; renting it from the Public Utilities for $15.00 per month. The size was about 40′ x 40′, 20 foot height, with a shack at the back that could be used for lumber. A great big belly-stove was supposed to keep it warm, but a far cry from it.

I moved all the machines into the new building with line shafts, pulleys and belts. Later on, the Public Utilities built a second floor which gave me double as much space for only $5.00 a month extra. The upper part I rented to one of my customers, Mr. Dick, for $20.00 a month, leaving me a little finishing space, and private living space; this way my rent was free. My motto is always "Keep overhead and expenses down."

A belt-sanding machine that I previously made in my previous building helped production a lot. After one and a half years, I bought two lots on Waterloo Street for $80.00 ($40.00 each) and drew building plans 40' x 50', two stories high. Another employee and I would make the foundation and do the carpenter work. Another employee from Europe was working on the windows to be used for the new factory. The blocks were laid by contract at a given price. This way I knew my cost. I bought all material. Half a year later the building was ready to move into. With all the lights on it looked like the White House, people would tell me. It was heated first by three stoves, later by furnace, and as time went on, by automotive oil burner. Sprinklers were installed to keep the insurance down. The original building cost me $4000 and taxes were $200 a year. The year was 1937. I paid $5 for a building permit.

Now that I had more and better equipment, I started to shift from making frames to making furniture, such as magazine racks and half-round end tables and furniture to order. The reason was more independence. I would make not less than 1,000 tables or magazine racks at a time, and sold the magazine racks for $1.00 to the furniture stores, and the tables from $1.25 to $1.50. As the years went by, I made larger and better tables, up to $20.00 each.

The original building we moved from Bridgeport Road on a lumber truck to my present lot, and placed it in the far left corner. In 1939 I built a shaving bin on the left side of the building. In 1940, war broke out. In 1943, I built a house on three lots at the corner. On the 25th of September 1943, I got married. The house was not quite finished so we lived for about a year and a half in the factory office where I lived before as a bachelor. In the spring of 1944, we moved into our new house, and about the same time I was drafted into the army for about 5 months until the end of the war in 1944.

After the war I built a new factory addition in 1945, in front of the old building: 75' x 35' with cement blocks faced with red bricks and large windows. Also, a 2-story building at a cost of $7,000.00.

In 1946 we replaced all old machines with new ones, as follows:

1. 4-sided sticker or moulder with 25 hp motor
2. 1 powered rip-saw—self-feeding 30 hp hm

3. 1 double cut-off saw, for straight & mitre cuts
4. 1 edgeband sander
5. 1 double belt sander
6. 1 trim saw with feeding slide bed
7. 1 router (used)
8. 1 cut-off saw or trim saw—foot pedal
9. 1 large compressor
10. 1 thickness planer
11. 1 new oil burner furnace
12. 1 homemade elevator
13. 1 complete machine room, conveyorized
14. 1 20 ft. hydraulic press, 6' high
15. 1 conveyorized finishing room
16. Shipping room, conveyorized in connection with the finishing line
17. 1 2-spindle horizontal drill (used)
18. 3 upright drill presses
19. 1 bandsaw (used)
20. Workbench with vise, bandsaw, sharpening machine, and drawer for machine parts
21. 1 large press, airpower driven, with 8 spindles
22. 1 long press, airpower for frames
23. 1 drawer press, airpower
24. 1 hydraulic forklift
25. 25 trucks
26. Complete office equipment
27. 1 pulley sander, soft, air-filled
28. 1 2-ft. diameter drum sander
29. 1 spindle shaper (homemade)
30. 1351 ft of storage conveyers
31. 1 electric grinder
32. All tools necessary for plumbing
33. Electric work and machine repair
34. Large selection of tools, knives and drills
35. Snowblower
36. 1 spray-booth & spray equipment with 6 spray guns
37. 6 pressure tanks
38. 1 hanger bolting machine, etc.

Alice was born in 1947 and Richard in 1950. As Richard grew up, he worked for me part time, and so did Alice. Richard was a good and reliable worker, and I hoped after his high school and Conestoga College attendance that he would enter into my business. I did not want to push him, but after working one summer for a building construction company, he finally came on strong and decided to work for me, which pleased me.

Alice entered into the hairdressing business, and after two years had her own business, doing very well because she was a good hairdresser.

During the time that Richard could not make up his mind which way to go, between Mounted Police, housebuilding, and furniture, I began slowing down, and instead of investing more money into the business as in the past, I built up my personal equity; however, when Richard in 1968 finally decided that he wished to work for me, was like a shot in the arm. From then on, we both were going in high gear—building up the business and sales.

In the meantime, I had made the private company into a limited company with common and preferred shares and gave Richard all the common shares; I retained all the preferred shares in order to have full control over the company. The reason that I gave Richard all the common shares was to protect him from a bad experience that happened to someone I knew. His father kept the common shares for himself, and on his death, the Tax Department demanded an enormous amount of taxes, but his son could not bring up the money, and therefore, was made bankrupt. The large 4-story factory with all its machines and equipment came under the hammer, and that was the last of it. The son himself went back to school and later became a schoolteacher instead. And I remembered, now that Richard's future was secure, and with father and son working harmoniously side by side, there was no reason that we should not double and triple our business in the future.

Richard was extremely good in sales and organizing, and I was good in the mechanized production, a good combination. Our further expansion required another addition to the factory, as we needed shipping and storage space, but that was the last we were allowed to build for lack of land.

Three quarters of the land was by now already built on. The next step would have to be moving to larger quarters.

In 1970, Richard got married and lived in a nearby apartment for 3 years. In 1973, Richard and Marilyn bought a new house on Academy Crescent, Waterloo. In 1977, we decided it was time to enlarge our business further; we wanted to buy a large panel saw, and in order to do that we required more space. We decided to buy the Electrohome plant in New Hamburg at a good price. The market was a buyer's market; however, what we lost on our factory in sale in Waterloo, we gained on the New Hamburg sale. The Waterloo factory was about 15,000 square feet in size, and the Electrohome factory was 30,000 square feet, plus a 5,000 square foot storage. So we moved, but not until we had set up our new plant. It looked desolate and empty at first, and Richard and I wondered whether we made the right decision at first. I must say it was a little scary for both of us at first.

The floors needed repairing. The storage building had to be fire-proofed in order to get a lower insurance rate. As a whole, the expenses were much higher than we were used to at our Waterloo plant on 142 Waterloo St. We decided that the only way to make it pay was to work hard and modernize by adding several most modern machines, such as panel saw, automatic double router, computerized, and Fletcher machinery.

Richard kept the factory in Waterloo going, and I started building a 130-pallet finishing line with 3 finishing booths. I had already started to lay out the plans at the Waterloo plant and had ordered the material. Since I never built a finishing conveyor of this kind before, I was a little nervous and asked myself, "Will it work or not?" It had to be ready at a given date and at times I worked nights until 2 o'clock, but finally it was completed. The 130-pallet conveyor with three spray booths worked like a charm. Later during the operation, I worked out further improvements.

In the meantime, we had installed the 29 machines and equipment from the old factory. One double-end tenoning machine was already in place, as we had bought it from Electrohome with the building. In the meantime, the new panel saw, taking up a large space, had come in from Italy. This machine would do 50 times as much production with one man, which we formerly did with four men on the trim saw. Later the 2-spindle automatic computerized router helped increase our production immensely. And when, finally, the Fletcher machine went to work, there was no stopping the production. It had to go up and up and it did. After the machines were all running, a tremendous upsurge of business took place, and why not?

The Fletcher machine also did wonders. It would shape any straight panel on both sides. At the same time, it would sand the mouldings smoothly and finally pressed a wood finished foil onto the moulding—all in one operation.

Our company was the second company in Canada that had purchased this fabulous U.S.A.-made machine. The only other company that had purchased this super machine was in Western Canada. Richard met the owner, who had received from the government the second honorary position of the whole furniture industry of Canada, and when he asked Richard, "I wonder who got the first?" Richard answered, "The Magnussen Furniture Co. did."

Right then and there, Richard could have sold our business at a handsome price, as the man was in the process of enlarging into Eastern Canada. But our factory at this time had all the modern equipment in the best shape and should each year double the production. So, it did pay off even with the larger overhead. But during the changeover the sales were lower. We asked the government for a 9% loan and received it. I had to put up my personal saving as security, but I was confident of our fiscal success, and with the new modern finishing line that I had installed for $10,000.00, which would have cost on the market at least $90 - 100,000.00, we should come out on top.

It was understandable that, during the year of change-over from one factory to the other, sales would be low, but now with completion of the super factory, sales went up and up, and doubled from year to year.

Within a year we had paid off our debt to the government, and when I left the factory for a good-earned rest, I left the factory as one of the most modern, well-equipped factories with no debts and money in the bank.

Further improvement in the form of equipment and building additions followed from year to year due to the influx of production, and this was only possible due to the efforts of Richard and I having undertaken the challenge of building a bigger and better mousetrap, if I may say so.

Before I left the factory for a good long rest, which I needed, we put Mr. Ed Lehmann in to take my place. He has the same qualifications that I have, experience, and was older than Richard with good factory learning, younger than I was, confident that he could take my place. He was younger than I, and over the years he proved it, and really did double the production from year to year as we had planned.

Our investment in a modern factory did pay off. At this point of change-over, I was 47 happy years in the furniture business, and Richard 12 years, and I think that I am entitled to a few years of rest, but that didn't stop me from keeping in touch with the factory.

I remember when I started during the depression with $365.00, and before

Richard's time, built up the equity 1,000 times its value. If I had spent the money for one year room and board, where would Richard and I have been today? I made the right choice, thanks to my fatherly wisdom, and I enjoyed it.

Richard is doing the same as I was doing before, only in a larger scale. He started where I left off. I am glad that I can share my business with Richard. He is entitled to it. Just because I worked 47 years until 1980, and he only 12 years, should not let that stand in our way of equal partnership. Where I have benefited him in the earlier years, he has benefited me later, with the help of Ed Lehmann. We all three expanded Magnussen Furniture into Magnum 11, etc. and added new additional building and equipment; also imported furniture. With this in mind, Richard not only received equal partnership from me, but also earned it, and I am glad that Ed could take my place and hope that he can stay until retirement and longer.

With the change of free enterprise between Canada and the U.S.A., we have to make drastic changes similar to what we did in 1979-80; but with the changes made within the next two to three years, we should come out with flying colors, as we did in 1979-80.

The impact of Free Trade will be so great that U.S.A. will flood our Canadian market at lower prices than we can produce. They already do so on a small scale.

For this tremendous change and upheaval, I like to be around and help Richard. For this reason, I would buy a condominium on the ground floor near Erb Street, Waterloo, and expedite a two-to-three-year plan from here. Since most people live here, it would be handy for occasional meetings, for which I would provide a meeting room, and separate office for myself, and office girl if necessary.

I would then concentrate on a two-to-three-year project of evaluation, information, and plans. Also, the import has to be carefully investigated. How long will it be profitable for Taiwan to supply us? Would it pay us to buy a U.S. firm on the Pacific Ocean for import? Will Taiwan raise the prices as Japan did over the years? We have to remember that Taiwan has to import all the oak veneer and solid oak and also all the plate wood from the U.S.A., only to be shipped back to us in knock-down (KD) furniture, and for us to assemble and place in cartons. For this reason, case goods and bedroom furniture would never pay to import from Taiwan. Therefore, it would have to be built in Canada on a large efficient scale, in order to compete with the U.S. This would require a super modern plant, German computer style. The advantage that we will have is to be selling to the American market with a population of 280 million people, plus 28 million Canadians.

To make this possible, a two-to-three-year research, evaluation, information, and plans would be necessary. I would be willing to put my services to work to find out what our competitors in North and South Carolina are doing. Their wages are less than ours in Canada and North America. Perhaps we could import some parts, and without paying duty, might be feasible. But basically, I don't believe that they are the only super race and with the same market available to us, we can do just as well; or maybe a little better.

We might even consider to let Taiwan's builder put up our super large building.

When in the spring of 1985 we put up a 20,000 square foot building, they put up a 40,000 square foot building for half the price. It would be worth Investigating. I was there in Taiwan. I saw the stone structure that they put up with a dome-type roof. Excellent!

To make all these changes and improvements gives me the adventure spirit, and I very much like to be around and duplicate what we did between 1977-80, but in a much larger scale with the inclusion of bedroom furniture.

A little adventure would be to me like a shot in the arm. Let's prove to the Americans and Europeans that Canada also can do a man's job.

This brings me to the conclusion of my story!

Thank you for bearing with me.

auf Wiedersehn.

Ingwer Magnussen

FAMILY BLESSINGS

For each of our children and grandchildren.
Life verses are all taken from the NIV.

OUR BLESSING
FOR KELLY AND KIM

Kelly and Kim, the evidence of your work ethic is clear to see in your family and your business. Those who know you best echo that observation. The testimonies at your twenty-fifth wedding anniversary brought tears of joy because of the reputation you have built for yourselves. So many of your friends attested to your respect in the marketplace and in the community. Your children are a testament to your values. They're not afraid of hard work or responsibility.

Kelly, you are our firstborn. We were overjoyed to have you as a son. That came with a lot of inexperience on our part as parents. But you survived. You make us proud because of the man, husband, father, and leader you have become. You are loyal, diligent, and lead with the highest level of integrity. Customers love you and so do your many friends.

Kim, you are fabulous; an amazing, supportive wife and mom. We love that you and Laura are best friends more than sisters-in-law. You have a passion for sports and, most of all, watching your kids as they compete in sports. We believe in you and your design business. You are loved by all because of your infectious personality.

Kelly and Kim, our dream for you is to grow in favor as good ambassadors of Christian grace and values in the marketplace and in your community.

LIFE VERSE: Numbers 6:24-25
The Lord bless you
and keep you;
²⁵ the Lord make his face shine on you
and be gracious to you;
²⁶ the Lord turn his face toward you
and give you peace.

OUR BLESSING
FOR TAYLOR

Taylor, you are our missionary. You chose to live in a community with others from your church for the purpose of sharing the gospel. The short-term mission trips you went on helped shape your passion and purpose in life. You have a heart for the things of God, and we can see you as the wife of some fortunate missionary or pastor. You are caring, patient, empathetic, and generous to the core. Bringing people together and providing hospitality is one reason everyone loves you. Your great sense of style, like your Nana's, led you to graduate from the Fashion and Marketing program at UNCG.

Taylor, our dream for you is to be a missionary in the marketplace and that your caring heart will continue to draw people to yourself as you live out being the hands and feet of Jesus.

LIFE VERSE: 1 Peter 4:10-11

Each of you should use whatever gift you have received to serve others, as faithful stewards of God's grace in its various forms. If anyone speaks, they should do so as one who speaks the very words of God. If anyone serves, they should do so with the strength God provides, so that in all things God may be praised through Jesus Christ. To him be the glory and the power for ever and ever.

OUR BLESSING FOR HAYLEY

Hayley, you stand quietly strong in adversity and under pressure. You played soccer for Wilmington University on a well-earned scholarship, and you were their highest scorer in your rookie year. In year two when the COVID vaccine came into effect and was mandatory for all players, you chose not to be vaccinated. You willingly stepped down from your scholarship and soccer team to be true to your convictions. We admire you for this.

You have always leaned into humility. In your high school, the previous day's sports accomplishments were announced throughout the school. Many times, you were honored. Everything about you is fast. You think fast on your feet. You are fast on the playing field. We see how ambitious you are. That's admirable. You worked as a nanny for three families AND a waitress to help put yourself through university. You are independent, excel at your schoolwork, and will be a woman who leads by conviction. Your empathy endears you to anyone you include in your life.

Hayley, our dream is for you to bring joy and peace wherever you work and wherever you live.

LIFE VERSE: Romans 15:13

May the God of hope fill you with all joy and peace as you trust in him, so that you may overflow with hope by the power of the Holy Spirit.

OUR BLESSING FOR BROOKLYN

Brooklyn, our favorite word for you is spicy! You bring joy and energy to every room, relationship, and family gathering. You are determined and ambitious. Your friendship is genuinely appreciated by all you gather in your circle. You are a wonderful nanny, appreciated by parents and loved by kids, all the while being diligent about getting your schoolwork done in university at Wilmington. You have a gift for sizing up situations and people and being very accurate. You are a risk taker with a successful, measured risk/reward thought process.

Brooklyn, our dream for you is to be a leader of many and that your life will be a testimony of Jesus's great love.

LIFE VERSE: Proverbs 3:5-6

Trust in the Lord with all your heart and lean not on your own understanding; in all your ways submit to him, and he will make your paths straight.

OUR BLESSING
FOR ALEXIS

Alexis, you are so much fun to be with! Joyful is an understatement. And that comes from being serious about life but not taking yourself too seriously. Your cheery attitude is a magnet for your younger cousins. You have an artistic flair and that's why studying cosmetology at Aveda College will create an opportunity for you to launch a career. Your sweet spirit will always open doors. Your ability in the kitchen shines when our family is together. Everyone enjoys your baking. People are attracted to you because you are a natural encourager.

Alexis, our dream for you is to have a great influence for Jesus in your hair salon and in the community through every day, positive, and meaningful conversations.

LIFE VERSE: Galatians 1:3-5

Grace and peace to you from God our Father and the Lord Jesus Christ, who gave himself for our sins to rescue us from the present evil age, according to the will of our God and Father, to whom be glory for ever and ever.

OUR BLESSING
FOR HAYDEN

Hayden, you are our scratch golfer. We see how well you apply yourself to your golf game, practicing all the time. You have a good way with people, like some of the older ladies at the golf club who are serious golfers and invite you to play a round with them. They appreciate that you can carry on a good conversation, and even when you often outplay them, they ask you to have lunch with them. We have to ask you how the game went because you never offer your score, especially when you win. Your humility is showing.

You are loyal, disciplined, and well-organized. You have a wise practice of saving your money and it's easy to see that you are meticulous when it comes to your personal space and possessions.

Hayden, our dream for you is that you would use sports as an opportunity to set an example that would draw people to Jesus.

LIFE VERSE: 1 Timothy 4:12

Don't let anyone look down on you because you are young, but set an example for the believers in speech, in conduct, in love, in faith and in purity.

OUR BLESSING
FOR LISA AND NATHAN

Lisa and Nathan, you have a vision for the family business and are working hard to ensure the foundation that was started in 1931 will continue to be a testimony in the marketplace. Your generosity is evident in so many ways. We see a deep gratitude to God in you that you have passed on to your children.

Lisa, you are our second born. We were thrilled at your birth. You possess a natural interior designer's eye. You are gifted with the ability to ensure that any home will be furnished well. Seeing pictures of your home published in a North Carolina magazine is just one piece of evidence of your remarkable talent.

Nathan, your knowledge of the furniture industry and your leadership ability has positioned the business for continued success. You have an incredible capacity to learn and are well liked in the industry. It would come as no surprise if you became president of the Home Furnishings Alliance.

Lisa and Nathan, our dream for you is that the family business will continue to be a beacon to the industry of how a high integrity business is conducted. We believe you will be ambassadors to draw people to Jesus because of your character and behavior.

LIFE VERSE: Philippians 4:19
And my God will meet all your needs according to the riches of his glory in Christ Jesus.

OUR BLESSING
FOR TY

Ty, you are a visionary. We admire your determination, intelligence, and leadership ability. Your decision to work at Magnussen Home in the distribution center reflects the savvy leader you are. We admire your decision to move up through the company so you could learn the business from the front line. Your smarts are beyond your years. For all the success you will have in business, keep your marriage the priority in your life. Making time for the things of God will always be a good investment.

Ty, our dream for you is to be godly and lead the home and furniture industry with great integrity and to share your faith by your actions.

LIFE VERSE: Ephesians 2:10
We are God's handiwork, created in Christ Jesus to do good works, which God prepared in advance for us to do.

OUR BLESSING
FOR GEORGIA

Georgia, you carry yourself with confidence. That takes humility. You are patient and flexible. Your disposition is incredibly sweet. People love being around you because you make everyone feel better about themselves. Your strong, quiet presence has a calming effect in any situation. When you speak, your words are wise and well-thought out. Your leadership abilities are clear to see. You know who you are and what you want. Your sense of the artistic will put you in high demand as a fashion expert.

Georgia, our dream for you is to be a great, living testimony of what it is to be a Jesus follower in the marketplace.

LIFE VERSE: Jeremiah 29:11,12

"For I know the plans I have for you," declares the LORD, "plans to prosper you and not to harm you, plans to give you hope and a future. Then you will call on me and come and pray to me, and I will listen to you."

OUR BLESSING FOR LAURA AND JOSH

Laura and Josh, we are impressed with your wisdom in relying on the Holy Spirit when you make decisions. You believed that God would open doors for the perfect job for Josh. You patiently waited for several years for the type of work he needed, trusting God for His timing. And God showed up. The perfect job came up in Raleigh, NC, and then you confidently waited an additional two years for the approvals and visa to work in the USA. We admire your patient trust in God. We see rich discernment and graciousness in you as a couple.

Laura, you are our last born. That came with more confident parenting practices and indescribable joy at your birth. We were over the moon for our third child. You are strong on administration and leadership. You manage everything well. As a leader you are respected and sought after in many areas, including school boards and church. You shine brightest in nurturing your children.

Josh, we pray for God's blessing in giving leadership on the home front and in your business. Your abilities have positioned you to become a trainer of trainers. We appreciate your demeanor because it is just what is needed to bring calm to some of our Magnussen chaos.

Laura and Josh, our dream for you is that God makes you great leaders and ambassadors for Jesus in your local church and community. Be willing to step into those roles as God opens doors.

LIFE VERSE: Joshua 1:9

Have I not commanded you? Be strong and courageous. Do not be afraid; do not be discouraged, for the Lord your God will be with you wherever you go.

OUR BLESSING
FOR BRODY

Brody, you have a million-dollar smile. You may not always speak first but when you speak your ideas are well thought out and worth listening to. You are a wise thinker because you think beyond the question. Your capacity for memory and recall is extraordinary. You are patient and possess an engaging sense of humor. Keep on writing. There is a gift there waiting to be explored at a deeper level. You have deep beliefs. Keep your focus on them so that they become convictions.

Brody, our dream for you is to grow into a man who leads by example and is known for peace.

LIFE VERSE: Philippians 4:9

Whatever you have learned or received or heard from me or seen in me—put it into practice. And the God of peace will be with you.

OUR BLESSING
FOR LOLA

Lola, you are always the first to be ready and waiting in the car to leave. No one needs to worry about you being late. In all your responsibilities, you get the job done well and timely. You are ambitious, generous, and tender-hearted. You excel as an equestrian rider and your ribbons attest to your exceptional abilities. When a group of people needs to be organized and led well, you ensure the group is efficient, focused, and successful.

Lola, our dream for you is to see you using your talents to become a life leader by example on getting things organized and achieving team goals.

LIFE VERSE: Philippians 4:6-7

Do not be anxious about anything, but in every situation, by prayer and petition, with thanksgiving, present your requests to God. And the peace of God, which transcends all understanding, will guard your hearts and your minds in Christ Jesus.

OUR BLESSING
FOR PAISLEY

Paisley, you have a tender heart. Caring for others is in your every heartbeat. You have made space for a marginalized or unpopular child in your class, and they became the center of your attention. You are a champion at helping them be seen and included. It is clear to people who know you best that you are confident and well-spoken beyond your years. We are amazed at how you can sit with people of all ages and engage them in enjoyable conversations like they are your peers.

Paisley, our dream for you is to use your sweet spirit and ability to communicate, to connect with many in a way that helps them hear the voice of Jesus.

LIFE VERSE: Psalm 100

Shout for joy to the Lord, all the earth. Worship the Lord with gladness; come before him with joyful songs. Know that the Lord is God. It is he who made us, and we are his; we are his people, the sheep of his pasture.

Enter his gates with thanksgiving and his courts with praise; give thanks to him and praise his name. For the Lord is good and his love endures forever; his faithfulness continues through all generations.

An intentional blessing is more powerful than an encouraging word. In their book, *The Blessing*, Gary Smalley and John Trent give five elements of a biblical blessing:

1. Appropriate meaningful touch
2. Spoken message
3. Attaching high value
4. Special future
5. Genuine commitment

"Every person needs the blessing to feel truly loved and secure about himself or herself." John Trent

- Have you ever received a blessing like this? How did it make you feel? Did it transform your life in any way? If yes, how?
- Have you ever given a blessing like this to someone? What did you tell them? How did the other person respond? Did it change their life in any way?
- Write a blessing for someone now. When and how will you share it with them? Will you speak it or give them a written letter? Will you include other elements such as Scripture or a prayer?

ACKNOWLEDGEMENTS

Thank you, Bob Jones, for how you have helped me express my thoughts. I enjoyed our many coffee times.

Creative, my publisher, for your many edits and the creativity to help my memoir come alive.

Thank you, Ken, for your Foreword to this book, as well as your friendship, leadership, and wisdom. I have learned so much from you.

Everyone who interviewed with Bob to help him gain a wider perspective on who I am and how I approach life, business, family, and faith.

AUTHOR BIOGRAPHY

Richard Magnussen, retired CEO of Magnussen Home, joined the family-owned company in 1970. He built one of the most aggressive global residential furniture companies, selling to more than 20 countries, finding homes for more than 150,000 pieces of furniture a month. Richard's focus on growth and expansion has driven Magnussen Home to become Canada's largest supplier with headquarters in North Carolina, corporate office in Ontario, and key distribution centres in California and HCMC Vietnam. Richard was the first Canadian chairman of American Home Furnishings Association (AHFA) and chairman of the board for Life Action Ministries USA. Richard resides in Waterloo, Ontario and winters in Naples, Florida with Marilyn, his best friend and wife of 53 years. He is proud of his three children and their spouses and is a champion of his ten energetic grandchildren.

www.ingramcontent.com/pod-product-compliance
Lightning Source LLC
Chambersburg PA
CBHW051339120626
46547CB00016B/2607